Spirituality

Part 1- Key to Physical and Mental Well-Being
&
Part 2- The Modern Perceptual Shift
(Preference for Emotional
Responses as Reality)

Dr Michael Gray

Author of, "To The Abyss (And How We Lost Touch
With Spiritual Living)" @ www.totheabyss.com

WESTBOW®
PRESS
A DIVISION OF THOMAS NELSON
& ZONDERVAN

WestBow Press books may be ordered through booksellers or by contacting:

WestBow Press
A Division of Thomas Nelson & Zondervan
1663 Liberty Drive
Bloomington, IN 47403
www.westbowpress.com
1 (866) 928-1240

ISBN: 978-1-4908-7786-0 (sc)
ISBN: 978-1-4908-7785-3 (hc)
ISBN: 978-1-4908-7784-6 (e)

Library of Congress Control Number: 2015906432

Print information available on the last page.

WestBow Press rev. date: 4/28/2015

Acknowledgements

To my Aunt Elsie, who was the first to take me to Church, thus beginning a spiritual journey that continues through to this day, and to my father, who instilled in me that God and Son matters.

Dedication

To my wife, Mary Carol, who has been my anchor
during my journey towards my Creator; who is my
motivation and the object of my dedications.

Contents

Part 2: The Modern Perceptual Shift
(Preference for Emotional-Responses as Reality)

Introduction to the Journey

It is customary to begin any literary effort with an explanation as to the reason or reasons behind writing the work and what the author's intentions were by exerting the effort to complete the book. What began as an observation, and later, an effort directed at accomplishing the goal of compiling a dissertation for a doctoral degree program, has led to this book's theme. Early on in the dissertation process, it became apparent to me that, in light of the present state of secular preeminence in this country, the topic of discussion was one that should be examined by society as a means of keeping traditional values of Western civilization pertinent and relative. Although the effort exerted may not be fully appreciated by a sizeable number of individuals, if it positively affects a portion of the public, it will have been worthy of the time spent in the writing.

This effort primarily consists of a revealing of the research on spirituality, particularly that of the past few years. The structure is loosely that of a compendium as it has the purpose of presenting the information that is available on the subject from a variety of sources and is brief. There are short and timely mention of the premises and points of interest from the subject research resources. I was initially concerned with preparing a lengthy and comprehensive volume that would be a long study. However, I came to realize that it is not the length of the book that will cover the topic, but the relevant, succinct coverage of the material that is all that is important. This being said, the book should have its value based upon the material within rather than the length and breadth of treatment of the topic.

As a revised and reprinted version, the book has benefited from my writing development to make the text more user-friendly. No matter what, or how much, is provided-if one does not profit from the material by being able to discern the text, it is of little use. I have attempted to address the terse and sometimes unwieldy previous writing attempt with a product that one can better appreciate. Further, a substantial revision has included what I feel is a fundamentally essential understanding of our world and the functional basis of humanity. This address to topic has a deeply important contribution to humanities awareness of our fragile and diminishing functional basis. In spite of what appears to be a clinical approach with a portion of Part 2; it is a vital read for practically anyone. Whether it is to understand our own functioning, that of our family members, or of society as a whole-the read is well worth the time and study. As such, it should be read with full attention and consideration.

In five years of work with at-risk youths in a residential training program, followed by fifteen years of work as a staff member of a mental health residential rehabilitation program working with veterans, it was apparent to me that those clients who presented as best disposed to their environment were those who professed a spiritual side to their being. Specifically, those who were most likely to recover from substance abuse were those who embraced and followed spiritual concepts and principles in their recovery. Those with a spiritual basis were least likely to present with behavioral problems. As a result of my work with the dissertation I was able to provide evidence of the value of spiritual living from a scientific viewpoint. The research work, when I measured spiritual levels and attempted a determination of a correlation between spirituality and abstinence, it provided significant findings. It was shown that the level of spiritual life was directly related to abstinence and recovery from substance abuse. In all but one instance, those who claimed abstinence also claimed to have experienced a spiritual awakening.

Let me be clear what I believe spirituality to be and what it is not. Gazing into crystals, hugging trees, being a member of a devil or demon worship group, or claiming there to be a Mother Earth are not spirituality as it is perceived by this writer for a few basic reasons. In most of these instances, one is worshiping the creation rather than the Creator, which I cannot support. Further, cultural epochs speak to a male deity known by many names, of which God is a preferred expression, to define that which is the Creator and traditionalist recorded history does not speak to a deity of the female gender as the Creator of humankind. Finally, that which seeks to destroy humankind without legitimate rationale is certainly not to be worshiped or revered. There are some entities that are perceived to be God that fail in this respect. Spirituality is, in essence, the relationship with a Creator as the believer understands him. Further, there is an active practice engaging in that relationship based upon recognition of the Creator as omnipotent, all-knowing, and most powerful.

Spiritual wellness is the derivative of spirituality and bears notice for its preventative and curative benefits. Spiritual wellness has been defined as consisting of four major themes.[1] Westgate wrote that the meaning and purpose to life, intrinsic values, transcendence, and the community of shared values made up the primary focus for spiritual wellness. Various other authors and thinkers have postulated other ways of approaching this principle; for example, saying that spirituality was associated with mind, body, and spirit. Some have settled on one or some of these concepts independently of the others. For this author, becoming aware of one's purpose, as prescribed by our Creator and attained through a personal relationship with that God, is the essence of spirituality. Living out that creed derived from this understanding is the relevance of our existence.

I was made aware in a perusal of the research literature that spirituality was correlated with positive results for a multitude of mental disorders such as depression, anxiety, and substance abuse (just to name a few). Spirituality was associated with successful management of symptoms from mental disorders. Likewise, spirituality was equally effective with assisting people with medical conditions. Much of what was seen as beneficial for spirituality was the existence of improved coping skills by those who practice a spiritual lifestyle. My reading provided me with an indication that spirituality was at the front of

---

[1]   C. Westgate, "Spiritual Wellness and Depression," *Journal of Counseling and Development* 75, (1996):26–35.

any discussion into a successful cure and return to functioning from a number of illnesses. It was apparent to me that how one approaches illness is key to successful recovery. In addition, a spiritual life leads to a reduction in the effects of the pressure of modern day living, with a relationship with a Creator taking the place of secular, material interests that are increasingly common.

In an age where a pill is seen as the cure to many conditions or, at least, used to mitigate the symptoms of mental or physical illness, it is refreshing to realize that a pill may not be the only, or even most effective, means of addressing dysfunction. As a mental health professional, I find that counseling, together with medication, is a successful combination that returns many to effective recovery from mental illness. The most effective or preferred approach is dependent on who you speak to concerning the relative merits of both counseling and medications. What few professionals are willing to address is the place of a spiritual relationship with a Creator in the remediation of illness.

This work aims to provide the evidence as to spirituality's importance for maintaining or returning from dysfunction to a healthy state of functioning. Evidence abounds concerning the benefits of the possession of a spiritual relationship, and this work will provide you with the summary of many of the assertions as to the benefits. At least, that is one of the primary purposes of this compendium of information on spirituality.

Lastly, the hope of this writer is that the evidence and information about spirituality, its benefits, and the present state of this personal state of being will be helpful to advance the importance of spirituality within the helping professions. As well, in the personal lives of the readers, I hope that it may provide the support and direction needed for engaging in the spiritual themes of humankind. The end being that the spiritual practice will make a difference for clients who are searching for meaning and purpose.

Certainly, Part 2 speaks of the therapy environment and provides a means of understanding the need for concerns being addressed separate of our present emotional context for functioning. The second part serves to provide a practical application to the theme of the first part of the book. In other words, the concentration on a reasoned, thought based-response found with logical-deduction is best developed with a foundation based on spiritual intelligence. This allows one to approach problems and define the logic to the issues in a manner that serves long-term benefits and existential issues. This is in comparison to an absence of the advantages of rationally-based awareness which being purely, emotionally "in the moment" fails to capture. I hope that you enjoy the read and find support to pursue an eternal association with your Creator. I believe that finding this personal relationship is infinitely more sustaining than the present secular-oriented social order.

-a servant,
"Dr. Mike"

Part 1

Spirituality: Key to Physical and Mental Well-Being

Chapter I

Defining Spirituality

Spirituality versus Religion

Various authors have made the clarification between religiosity and spirituality.[1] They state that this clarification involves a differentiation between established practices, such as affiliation and involvement with a particular religious group, and private importance given by the individual to religious tenets to define religiosity. A personal transcendent experience that often includes inquiry, examination, growth, and change is a means of defining spirituality. This process may also said to occur with an adherence to religion on the individual level. Spirituality has been explained as consisting of a "self-transcendence within or apart from a religious setting"[2] with the recognition of the existence and omnipotence of a higher power. It is seen as the act of having a relationship with this entity as necessary to have a spiritual relationship.

Jarusiewicz referred to Miller's clarification between religion and spirituality as the difference between a "social phenomenon" [and an] "ideographic aspect of the person."[3] The one (religiosity) is an organized group activity whereas the other (spirituality) is an individual, personal relationship that follows the parameters of the individual practicing it.

It bears noting that with religiosity, there are traditions, ceremonies, rituals, and a group dynamics of associations to include group study of the texts and precepts associated with the religion. It also includes a group assemblage to share in common beliefs. With spirituality, there is the individual who is in a relationship with God on a one-on-one basis (although some religions have many deities). In one's spiritual relationship, one gives allegiance to and efforts at obedience to that Creator who serves as the focus of the relationship for the spiritual experience. These make up the common variation between religion and spiritual experiences.

Another equally telling variation between religion and spirituality is the lack of guidance for the one versus the overwhelming direction that is often present in the other. With spirituality, one is involved in a relationship free of interference or inference as to what is acceptable or permissible. With religion, there are basic tenets that one is expected to adhere to within the practice of the faith. It is entirely possible to have the spiritual experience within any environment or through multiple mediums. In comparison, religion often has elaborate buildings or structures as a central meeting place for those like-minded people who share the same regard for how and what to practice as religion. One can have as much (or as little) ritual and ceremony involved within the spiritual experience as one desires, while an established pattern of worship is provided by the religious denomination (churches) to which the individual has an allegiance. It is not just the environment or ceremony that sets the two at variance, but also the schedule, structure, or restrictions placed on behavior that separate the two.

Those involved in religious practices usually have a specific time to assemble for worship, bible study, prayer, or fellowship that is prescribed based upon the religion or denominational restrictions. Muslims have specific times of the day that they enter the mosque with the intention of praying. For Protestants, Sunday is a historically acceptable day for worship. It appears reasonable to consider that these time-specific practices are a result of attempting to place the worship convenient to the many other secular responsibilities that an individual must attend to on a daily and weekly basis. With spirituality, the individual may make time for the development and refinement of their spiritual existence without a set time or place for practice. However, what they practice is just as important as when or where they do so.

A mosque, church, synagogue, or sanctuary is the prescribed location for most religious practices without many alternative locations for the practice of the religious faith. The obvious exception to this is found with prayer, which allows for the practice before meals, at bedtime, or other chosen moments in the daily life of the believer (this may concurrently be seen as spiritual). This being said, religion finds that its' predominate place of practice of worship to be in a building designed for that purpose. Spirituality is a practice that is equally at ease in a field, forest, on water, on land, or in the solitude of wherever the individual may be at the time of the self-felt need to commune with the Creator. Some spiritually-led individuals may have a preferred place to practice their spirituality, but there are no actual restrictions or restraints based upon location.

Religion is not only a means of worship of the Creator, it also directs the activities and practices of the individual as to diet, the concept of family, paying of taxes, belief in government, and a host of other aspects of the civilized experience of all individuals on the planet. Just because one does not profess to be governed by religious practices does not mean that they are not, in fact, governed by them. Scriptural references are made of many concepts and traditions that find their place in the everyday life of practically all individuals.

The formation of family and government with the payment of taxes and allegiance to government leaders is found in religious scriptures. The avoidance of certain foods or liquids (e.g., pork or alcoholic beverages) is a direct result of religion and religious precepts. For many years, the United States (particularly in the South) had what were entitled "blue laws" that forbade stores from operating on Sunday. That day was set aside as it was seen as a traditional day of religious worship. Spirituality, on the other hand, is not as formalized and allows for the flexibility of each individual placing their own prohibitions or restrictions on their behavior as they feel led.

In this respect of the effects on the lives of populations, it can be argued that religion is a component, actual embodiment, or a separate part of culture. Some peoples are identified by their religion while others are understood by the application of religious principles and stories. Still other individuals may be seen as a distinctive segment apart from the general population of a region by their religion and practice of that religion.[4] In these instances, culture is defined by understanding the religion of the people. Religion is so all-encompassing that it embodies what the people of a region stand for, believe in, and behave in accordance with. Consequently, the different denominations of the United States are identified by their rituals and means of the practice of their cultural identity.

When one practices one's faith or spirituality, there are differences that are particularly telling. For example, in the Catholic Church (as in many others as well), there is a rigid structure to the worship. This is even to a point of dictating what the individual will speak as a response to the clergy leading the service. Traditionally, one is expected to dress in a reverent manner and maintain a solemn and reserved demeanor in many religious settings. Particular individual or individuals are responsible for leading the remainder of the congregation in the worship process. With a spiritual relationship, one is free to speak in the manner that reflects what is in one's heart and on one's mind, without being led or directed by another. The relationship is between the one practicing the spirituality and the Creator—without an intercession.

Still others differentiate between religions as being distinct variants of a vertical religion versus a horizontal religion.[5] This view equates a vertical religion with the relationship of the individual with God, and a horizontal religion with the relationship of the individual and society (social connectedness), in so many words. A vertical religion is more practically seen by this writer as being spirituality in its basest form. It involves providing one's own efforts to go it alone in one's quest to develop understanding of the meaning and purpose of life and in one's connection to their God.

When one looks at other equally confusing explanations for spirituality then there is the one that states spirituality can be epitomized by five concepts. These concepts do not speak to a Creator or a relationship within the cosmos with one.[6] It readily becomes apparent that the lack of consensus of exactly what spirituality or religion is may be a prime rationale that such confusion exists over either of these formless gifts.

Not only is there confusion as to what religion and spirituality are, there is also a lack of effort to achieve the fullest level of commitment. Many see religious and spiritual practices as rote exercises without personal meaning or reward. This is a question of motivation and commitment for either spirituality's or religion's sake or of motivation for and commitment to one over the other. Although one who maintains membership with a denomination or particular religious group is dedicated to various degrees, one who is involved in a genuine and sincere quest of a spiritual nature must be motivated and driven to delve deeply into the relationship with a Creator.

In both religion and spirituality, one must be dedicated to the practice to be highly effective. With religion, one can lean on fellow parishioners or a clergy member whereas this may not be available for one who is of a solely spiritual nature in their relationship with a Creator. Therefore, it may be posited that one must be disciplined to be a truly spiritual creature—more so than one who claims religious affiliation only. While there is a distinction in this discipline and motivation factor, they sometimes are blurred without a clear boundary between religion and spirituality. The divergence in means of discipline can be seen in the difference in adherence to prescribed customs and ceremonies that are expected to be adhered to versus the discipline of maintaining a piety with faith for spiritual concepts and principles. These concepts may be value-oriented, or moral and ethical considerations for the connectedness between the created and across societal lines.

It has been my experience that those individuals who are spiritual may, or may not, be religious. However, at least initially, an indoctrination into religion principles prior to the development of a spiritual basis for faith usually occurs. It seems only reasonable to assume that one must be aware of the presence of a Creator before one can embark on a journey of discovery to engage in a relationship with the Creator. In order to pray, one must be at least rudimentarily aware of the general principles behind prayer. In order to practice meditation, some training or instruction must have occurred—whether it is in reading a manual or going to a religious assemblage.

So, it seems practical to assume that most individuals who practice a degree of spirituality first began with a religious indoctrination from some source in order to be cognizant of the existence of a Creator and of the basic practices of spiritual living such as prayer and meditation. It has been estimated that a significant portion of what is considered spiritual has its origins in religion, but this is only relative to what is practiced by that person who professes and follows spiritual principles. Much of what, if spiritual, may be seen as a quest for understanding of our purpose, meaning, relationship with God, and affiliation with our fellow human beings who share the world with us.

The real problem, and an important reason for the existence of a spiritual experience, is that many individuals have been drawn away from religion due to the inference associated with what is acceptable and expected of the individual. This is not to suggest that those things expected are harmful or detrimental to the individual in any measureable way; on the converse, they are often beneficial. Also, this does not mean that a spiritual experience is not a natural extension of many religious lifestyles; however, I have heard many people claim to be spiritual, but not religious, due to the limitations and expectations that religion places on the individual. The spiritual individual may be an individualist apart from social convention, which is a driving rationale behind the selection of spirituality over religion.

As has been discussed, the family, government, taxes, food and drink, and many other aspects of life are dictated by religion and based upon religious texts and religious leaders. People have, often, become disillusioned due to these restrictions or what they view as hypocritical personalities associated with religion. There is a definitive advantage to spirituality; no one is imposing any expectations or guidelines on the way one lives nor are there obligations beyond that which the individual feels compelled by their conscience to adhere to. What I have experienced in my own spiritual walk is that many precepts associated with religion are instinctually followed due to the perceived "rightness" of them, and religion does not have a place in guarantee of my compliance to them, they only seem proper through rational logic and meditation.

It is of importance to further mention those which are considered hypocritical personalities of some religious leaders, as they live in mansions and have private airports with jets while receiving monies from a national audience for their ministry. These individuals may be pious and full of personal integrity, but their wealth brings consternation to many who use this as a reason for their lack of religious participation. The question here is, "How can one lead others in a journey of discovery of the Creator when they profit from the wealth of their supporters and live lavishly as a result of their name and position?" Many of these leaders have gotten their wealth from book writing or speaking engagements, but this is not considered by the average American who only sees that this individual, from a particular church, is living lavishly.

The disdain for those who have been financially rewarded while serving as heads of church bodies is the central reason for the focus on spirituality by a number of those who prefer spirituality to religiosity. With the wars and terror that have been propagated in the name of religion, it can be understood as a reason for the avoidance by others from a religious experience. These individuals trust their own efforts at finding truth and developing faith, as compared to following a clergy that is, in many cases, as hedonistic and materialistic as those who do not practice any faith. It is not the intention of this writer to judge the merits of the feelings of these people or whether it is morally sustainable to derive financial profit for work associated with religion; that is a matter of conscience for the individual—both the religious leader as well as the potential parishioner.

An important consideration must be registered as to the good aspects of religion as well as for most participants; it is not about mega-church personalities, but the community pastors who tend loyally to their flocks. Those who actively participate in religious experiences are much more likely to avoid dangerous and risky behaviors. They do not, as a whole, engage in criminal activities, avoid drug and alcohol dependency and abuse, and typically have a lower level of excitement required to be satisfied with their lives. The practice of religion is associated with longer life as lifestyle considerations are more conservative and concerned with keeping the temple (i.e., the body) clean. Whereas religion is man-made and human directed, the journey to which it leads the individual is usually involving a spiritual connection and a quest for spiritual principles that may coexist with religion or develop in the absence of continued religious participation.

Religion is seen as being made up of four "dimensions" that include the concepts of "believing, bonding, behaving, and belonging."[7] Those who practice religion can be epitomized as being observant of a higher standard than many in society. This is common in regards to morals and behaviors while being disposed to community and other locally-based interests. They see themselves as belonging to something higher-ordered than a government and obligated to seek purity in their daily lives. Again, it is significant to accept that the human element of that religious practice may lead to excesses that religion seeks to avoid and control.

Religion can be seen as a search for connectedness with community, just as spirituality is the outgrowth of that connectedness that creates a personal relationship or connectedness with God. The need to belong to something greater than ourselves encompasses the need to coexist in a religious community as much as it does to have that intrinsic personal relationship. Religion is adequately explained as the fuel and spirituality is seen as the result of the expending of that fuel. Whereas one may see themselves as being spiritual; it is doubtful that there was not, at a minimum, a religious experience that predated that spirituality.

It is my goal, when working with clients who are interested in leading a spirit-filled life and following spiritual principles, to encourage them to first understand the relative merits of both religion and spirituality. From there, the attempt follows to form reasonable expectations of each for their lifestyle. Religion has been at the center of wars and conquests for the sake of faith, it has been the source of support and guidance for the masses, and there are instances of abuses towards individuals just as there are times when the needs of the downtrodden have been resolved. The caveat for religion is that it is designed and carried out by man and nothing that man has ever designed or carried out is remotely perfect or without significant flaw and error.

This is not to say that spirituality is without concern; many will aimlessly go about a quest for understanding of their Creator's intentions for their life for some time before they settle on what the actual purpose of their life is. One writer stated that a caveat to spirituality was the adherence to distinctly different and incongruent ideals from a variety of religious sources that leads to less than an ideal meaning to life.[8] The difference between spirituality and religion is that, with spirituality, the individual is responsible for what they make of their relationship with their Creator and it is not determined from their adherence to others' direction and guidance. Spiritual individuals will not have the support of social convenience, but they may have the freedom to express themselves to their Creator that they feel led to do without being chastised or ridiculed by a more traditionalist means of spiritual expression found with orthodoxy.

A final mention must be made of the propensity to see things as spiritual when they do not conform to the traditionalist definition forwarded by this discourse. Much mention is made in literary circles of spiritual this and spiritual that, yet there is a failure to mention a relationship between the individual in question and any Creator in many instances. Instead, music, literature, and daily activities are seen as "spiritual" when this perverts and dilutes the meaning and essence of the spiritual experience that allows personal growth and the connectedness to something greater than oneself. Still others suggest that we look at each religion individually as a separate entity in forming our understanding of spirituality and religion. [9]

In doing research, I am struck by the loose interpretations provided for the principle of spirituality, and an even greater misguided aspect involving the presentation of spirituality is occurring within the past decade. It is perhaps this loose and disjointed defining of spirituality that led one writer to observe that spirituality allows one to avoid having a meaningful relationship with God. He stated that spiritual people failed to see the gifts to humanity that religion has offered over history.[10]

As academics seek to investigate and define spirituality, they utilize the scientific method to analyze the impact and effect of spirituality on a host of life events or issues. Trying to determine and define spirituality based on number crunching and research paradigms does not fulfill the essence of spirituality. Nor does it take into account the texts of religious dogma upon which a large volume of the beliefs associated with spirituality are derived. I venture to state that many of those who are investigating spirituality and its effects do not have the a priori knowledge of religious texts to understand the principles and guiding traditions associated with the concept. Failure to have this understanding dooms their research to be shallow and lacking in the authenticity. This is in comparison to that which is found with someone who can provide the basis for the attributes associated with the concept of spirituality.

Chapter II

Measuring the Presence of Spirituality

——◦◦——

Attributes Associated with Spirituality

In discussions between this writer and many others who profess a spiritual awareness/connectedness, there seems to be an ordering to the concepts that make up spirituality. Some concepts appear almost universal, such as the existence of a Creator and individual guidelines such as the sanctity of life. Other universal concepts include a belief in an improved hereafter beyond this existence and the unification of the individual with the Creator in that afterlife. Other concepts are not as universal, as diverse beliefs and practices are associated with spirituality. The concept of spirituality is therein seen by many in different manners and defined divergently.

Shorkey, Uebel, and Windsor determined that the use of a measure of spirituality must address an awareness of spiritual aspect(s) of reality, perception/awareness of God, belief that God mediates outcomes in everyday life, a personal spiritual experience determines interactions with God, perception of characteristics and quality of interaction with God, a relationship with God that produces positive attributes in emotion, cognitions, and behaviors related to self, others, and the world, and a relationship with God that produces a sense of well-being.[11]

Johnson et al. stated there are five dimensions to the measure of spirituality that must be considered which are "religious/spiritual involvement, search for meaning, religious struggle, quest, and spiritual well-being."[12] A pragmatic definition of spirituality, beyond these proposed theoretical bases, includes multiple potential examples of what spirituality actually encompasses. It is important to acknowledge the idea that spirituality can be subjective in the sense of consisting of experiences and examples that are peculiar to each individual. As such any author's assertion of addressing the factors presented are but one interpretation of the essence of spirituality.

Some see spirituality as a collection of emotions. Vaillant indicated that eight emotions were at the core of spirituality. These emotions were "awe, love, trust (faith), compassion, gratitude, forgiveness, joy and hope."[13] The impression gained from a consideration of this definition of spirituality is that these traits or qualities represent the Creator, but these traits, in and of themselves, do not completely encompass the totality of the practice or act of living a spiritual lifestyle. They are certainly important considerations for any discussion of spirituality, but mere words sometimes seem inadequate to describe the spiritual experience of the individual when left to being described by trait features. These factors are possibly identified with the "virtue" of a previous age when many virtuous aspects associated with conduct were common study for personal social development. It appears reasonable to conclude that these "virtues" have been debunked and discarded by observation of present social culture for a majority of the inhabitants.

Ellison and Fan broke down the spiritual experience into examples of what one means by the spiritual experience.[14] The experiencing of God in the individual's life (through others, self, and in close proximity to the individual), finding solace within religion and religious experiences, and experiencing inner peace and satisfaction with life were an initially expressed explanation. Additionally, feeling a connectedness to God (and others) as well as accepting life without reservations represent the examples provided within the test of the Daily Spiritual Experience

Scale (DSES) that Ellison and Fan utilized to ascertain the existence of a spiritual experience for their research.

Others have suggested that an acknowledgement of the existence of God, the unity of nature and life, or a connectedness with all humans across multiple generations are aspects that represent as spiritual in nature.[15] Neff and MacMasters provided that the existence of daily spiritual experience(s), values and beliefs, forgiveness, and positive religious coping as indicative of spirituality;[16] whereas Stewart, Kieske, and Pringle pointed to the meaning [of life], guilt, and a loving/forgiving God to be measurements of spirituality.[17] Kendler indicated the additional factors of "unvengefulness" and thankfulness as components of spirituality.[18]

So that there is a lack of confusion, understand that all of the factors thus far attributed to being spiritual are but a partial list based upon life experience, study, and observation in most instances. Any one of us may do similar activities and provide the evidence from personal effort to understand this principle (spirituality) yet, ultimately, the success of the personally-led spiritual existence will be the gold standard of fully understanding its' essence. Spirituality appears to be something that is only fully appreciated by practice of it.

The potential means of measuring these factors appears limitless, and the tabulation and compilation to arrive at the results are equally controversial. What weight does one give to each aspect described? Which ones are the most universal in value and which ones are the least important? How does one go about categorizing these qualities if spirituality is understood in domains and sub-domains? There appear to be some key category identifications that many tests have provided to conceptualize what spirituality consists of. They include the categories of spiritual well-being, spiritual control, and spiritual experience. There are undoubtedly many more ways to view the spirituality categories with a wide divergence in opinion (such as Kim's spiritual orientation).

Kim felt that spirituality in the workplace involves acceptance that we are all interconnected and made up more of unknowns than what is known. We are also capable of becoming complete through active thought, can change our condition, and have our greatest power in a collective consciousness.[19] Whereas these concepts serve as a springboard for further considerations, they do not make up a manifesto in and of themselves. They fail to be a separate, stand-alone theory and suggest that their utility lies in pondering the existence of the Creator. He alone is identified with creating all spiritual concepts rather than as a separate source of a spiritual explanation.

This is a common fallacy with many modern spirituality models and the question needs to be asked in all instances in which one claims spirituality models or theories—where is their source and from what do they claim the rightness to their consciousness? Some see stretching exercises know as yoga as being spiritual. Others state that viewing a beautiful vista is a spiritual experience for them. Without a Creator, the spirituality loses its flavor and moral compass.

Pepper, Jackson, and Uzzell stated that the understanding of the attributes of spirituality versus those of religion involves a consideration of the differences between emotion and personal experience for spirituality versus the traditions and collectivism of religion.[20] Self-transcendence and self-enhancement are at the center of spirituality, whereas institutionalism and conservation are associated with religion, the authors suggest. Finally, their research results indicated that the greatest values associated with the joint construct of religion and spirituality was that of benevolence and less so with self-direction or hedonism. Although hedonism had been theorized to be the least attributable value to the joint construct of religion/spirituality, self-direction was even less likely as a value associated with the joint constructs of religion and spirituality. In a nutshell, the idea is that pleasure related behaviors and independence without collectivism of the created are both detrimental to the joint concerns for spirituality and religion.

On a more general basis, attributes associated with spirituality include being intensively alive and complete. In doing so it is inferred that they have discovered the purpose of their life having had the transcending experience. Wills posited the idea that the individual who had a spiritual existence was satisfied with life and had a higher level of self-actualization than was otherwise attained by someone without this experience.[21] Wills also stated that "in a eudaimonic approach to happiness, satisfaction with spirituality is understood as the transcendent dimension that deals with the ultimate goal in life and gives meaning to existence."[22] This was implied with a statement of a spiritual existence serving to satisfy human potential in another portion of his research article.

Rican and Janosova have suggested that spirituality is a separate and distinct part of the personality of the individual (universally) across cultures.[23] They referred to work done to follow up on that by Piedmont and stated that prayer fulfillment, universality, and connectedness were attributes of spirituality separate from those that were found in other scales associated with personality. These attributes were suggested by the authors to have an effect on the individual's attitudes towards the central issues of our time (such as abortion) as well as prosocial behavior and vulnerability to stress. It is being suggested that attitudes to these and other questions are ingrained into personality rather than being the source of reflection. It was theorized that one comes to an understanding of what they mean to the individual on a spiritual level of inquiry. This research would suggest that we are born as spiritual beings and have the presence of a spiritual existence as an element of our existence.

However, the antithesis to spiritual attributes is the common state of boredom.[24] In this view, a lack of spirituality and, more specifically, a lack of purpose to life is the medium within which boredom exists. With the dire results to such a psychological state it appears significant to assess whether the problem has its origins with the family or the larger community, including schools and other institutions to which the individual is exposed.

Test Measurements

Equally complicated as the task of defining spirituality, the means by which this concept is measured is not definitively determined by a specific, universal test measure or inventory. Hill and Hood reviewed over 120 test measures for religiosity and spirituality and the list has continued to grow since that time.[25] Gorsuch theorized that a major problem with the measurement paradigm is "whether religiousness should be thought of as a [one] dimensional or a multidimensional construct."[26] The inference here is that one could look at religion based on total obedience with all people falling short as scripture suggests, or by measuring adherence and compliance to various categories of the religious experience (food laws, family cohesion and compliance with elder's directions, obedience to the absolute religious tenets, etc.) and the individual passing some tests, but being deficient on other categories.

Since none are blameless or without shortcomings, it seems appropriate to see the measurement of spirituality and religiosity as being linear. It is reasonable to conclude that there is a progression of scoring with low, moderate, and high score attainment possible for each person. This would be in spite of their actual, conscious practice when preliminary spiritual intelligence had been developed as a youth and inserted into dealing with life issues. In the instances where there is no a priori training, scores for the various measured traits would seem to more often clustered around the middle to low, or middle to moderate, ranges. It would appear to be difficult to demonstrate that which was not known or from which training had not been given.

The literature thus far provided also includes the suggestion that there is a "latent" quality to spirituality as a moderator of behavior. This would imply that multiple domains and sub-domains must also be considered in the measurement of the component parts that spirituality consists of within the individual test participant whose spirituality level is being measured. This suggestion also goes to act of using a category concept of division into workable entities for the complicated and comprehensive possibilities associated with daily living such as work, play, school, and church (just to name a couple of possibilities) that spirituality oftentimes provides experiences within.

Further complicating the attempt to measure the essence of spirituality results when subjective concepts are under consideration (such as quality of life) or the measurements of spiritual domains. (Examples of the domains include experience, control, or well-being which are considered when measuring the presence or absence of spirituality.) Another question is by whose standards are these domains or sub-domains established? Who are the actual authorities on spirituality?

And a serious question to be answered is, "From where does spirituality come?"

Some have stated that spirituality is an integral part of personality and, as such, is with us from birth. Others speak to a form of intelligence that must be developed whereby we are able to see things in human, existential fashion. Still others promote the notion that spirituality is learned from nothingness much like the blank slate of humankind at birth which has the principles of spirituality burned into the psyche during development. This would conform to the psychological principle of a blank slate that is how our brain, at birth, is described. Regardless of from where it arrives, it is measureable by a plethora of test measures.

Shorkey et al. selected 10 test measurement scales and inventories that have utility in the measurement of spirituality, which they surmised to be the most effective means of measuring the domains associated with spirituality.[27] These tests, as their titles indicate, cover domains associated with spirituality such as (a) Belief in Personal Control, (b) Daily Spiritual Experience(s), (c) The Spiritual Health Inventory, (d) Spiritual Well-Being Scale, (e) Orientation Toward Religion and Spirituality Index, (f) Spirituality Self-Assessment Scale, (g) Spirituality Scale, (h) Index of Core Spiritual Experience(s), (i) Spiritual Assessment Inventory, and (j) The Spiritual Belief Scale.[28] It is suggested that these test measures identify and score attributes associated with the possession of the essence of spirituality by the test taker. Further, these domains are suggested as being appropriate indicators of the possession of spirituality.

What is apparent from this listing of test measures is that personal control, spiritual experience, spiritual health and well-being, spiritual beliefs, spiritual practices, and self-perceptions of spirituality growth and existence are all valuable parts of the overall study of spirituality. It is as important to consider spiritual beliefs as it is to study spiritual practices. Likewise, it is also as meaningful to assess present existence versus the growth and development with respect to the spectrum of spiritual issues. As the ultimate goal of a spiritual relationship is to become closer to the Creator, it seems relevant to assess the health and well-being of the spiritual experience that the person is presently having as well. The final goal and ultimate questions is, "Have they achieved nirvana?"

Another measure for spirituality is the Higher Power Relationship Scale, which has applications for measurement of AA (Alcoholics Anonymous) affiliation and relationships with a Higher Power. The designers of this test took great effort to ensure there was a differentiation between religion and spirituality within the test material by including both references to God and the Higher Power within the response questions. This was so that they could have applicability to a broad cross-section of potential test participants who may be secularly inclined.[29] All of these test measures can be utilized to address AA/NA (Narcotics Anonymous) conceptual spirituality as it relates to the substance abuse treatment field with the 12-step AA/NA model. The specific inferred results of higher scores on these tests include having a personal belief of high levels of personal control and spiritual wellness. Also, satisfaction with the way that their life was being lived and a feeling of connectedness with the Creator are personally felt beliefs as well. Finally, they feel that they are possessing an experience of living a life intertwined with that of God as they understand him. It appears that these inferred results of high scores are indicative of what constitutes the possession of spirituality. It appears that these inferred results of high scores are indicative of what constitutes the possession of spirituality. The central tie-in to spirituality in these instances includes an inclusion of God to the equation for spiritual development.

Of the test instruments available to measure various dimensions of religiosity and spirituality, the Spiritual Health Inventory (SHI) has been recognized for psychometric reliability and validity for the measurement of spirituality within three dimensions (Spiritual Experience, Spiritual Locus of Control, and Spiritual Well-Being).[30] In their evaluation of the SHI, Shorkey et al. stated there was validity for a number of scales associated with the well-being and they include attention to depression, substance abuse, and the overall physical state of the client taking the inventory.

Of note is the fact that the self-rating health scale was found to be useful in differentiating groups at different lengths of recovery. Also important to consider in the use of the SHI is that the longer the recovery, the prediction is that the internal spiritual well-being will also be higher. It is suggested that the higher score on the spiritual well-being scales, the greater sense of having, or having had, a spiritual experience, greater spiritual locus of control, and greater spiritual well-being.[31] These three aspects or dimensions of the Spiritual Health Inventory serve to highlight whether there is a relationship with God, and by how much a person has the experience of having a God as a part of their life in a meaningful manner.

The personal determination of the personal value assigned to that relationship by the individual is assessed by these dimensions as well. The circumstances surrounding the events in the person's life are measured by the self-report of the client on the inventory. They consider whether the client sees these events as mere chance (fate), or whether they are at the direction of a Creator or God. Finally, the personal assessment that the test taker has about their relationship to the world, whether they are in sync with the world, and if they are fulfilling their purpose or meaning to life as they believe it to be are just some of the perceived, measured dimensions within the SHI. Although this is a tall order, the test has given indications of being able to accomplish an assessment of the level of spirituality of the test taker quite effectively.

Having used the SHI for research, I can attest to the validity and reliability of the test instrument as the subject questions making up the instrument cover the essence of spirituality from a practical standpoint. Common, everyday things such as habits of reading religious texts, going to church services, and talking to God make the test relative to many Americans to ascertain the level of and existence of a spiritual lifestyle.

Test measures also measure spirituality and religion from a standpoint of these variables in relationship to other concepts—subjective well-being (SWB) is but one example of a concept that incorporates the spirituality and religion domains as a part of the whole of SWB.[32] The development of the SWB test measure revealed that a domain that accounted for spirituality and religion was significant as a factor leading to the subjective well-being of individuals. This is evidenced by behaviors exhibited by individuals who attended church in Western countries.

As one leafs through the barrage of potential test measurements that are available, it is remarkable to see that many, if not most, have a domain of the overall test measure to account for spirituality. The key to understanding of these test measures is that some actually recognize spirituality as consisting of multiple domains. The address of spirituality by MacDonald saw the resultant research indicating that there were five dimensions to the Five Factor Model of spirituality. He developed a measure that he named the Expressions of Spirituality Inventory, which consists of 98 items.[33] This test measure finds application that form comparisons to the Five Factor Model of personality. What MacDonald attempted to do was provide a test measure that more adequately measures the essence of spirituality by adding clarity to the identity of spirituality, which he hoped to accomplish with five factors being identified as the components of spirituality rather than seeing spirituality as one dimensional.

Chapter III

Spirituality and Substance Abuse Recovery

Spirituality and AA/NA

Substance abuse treatment is complicated by multiple factors to consider. Motivation to participate and demonstrate ability to engage the participants once they accept and become committed to participate are key concerns. Choice of the appropriate model of treatment dependent upon the needs of the client and the use of the tools that are of the most help to ensure recovery are also considerations. Determining the best practice for substance abuse treatment has not been definitively ascertained, as various large and comprehensive studies have been unable to isolate a preferred method or delivery of that method for elevated success rates. The data, as applies to success rates, participation rates until completion of treatment, and regarding the extent of substance abuse is problematic. Low success rate statistics, abbreviated participation failing to complete treatment, and diminished significance of therapy by those being served are all issues. The statistics and potential results associated with substance use and abuse in society and the success rates are dismal and discouraging.

Psychotherapy does not appear to be effective for substance abuse, according to Vaillant's Harvard University study of 26 men who received, on average, 200 hours of psychotherapy per participant with one participant recovering from alcoholism.[34] Vaillant stated that disulfiram has failed to cure alcoholism, acamprosate and naltrexone have not had long-term studies conducted to determine if they contribute to the remission of alcoholism after 15 years of use in treatment. These medication treatments are often ineffective as the patient frequently ceases taking the prescription due to unwanted side-effects. Further, incarceration has not been shown to remediate substance use as self-reporting of many former inmates attests to the ready availability of illicit substances within prison facilities. This is in spite of staff efforts to monitor inmate's incoming mail, packages being passed during visitation, or unobserved interactions between inmates.

In getting to the point of abusing substances or a dependency on those substances, the individual must first have the desire to use in practically any case. This refers to the principle of cravings as they are called in the substance abuse treatment field (among others). Mason et al. stated that spirituality may actually reduce the cravings associated with substance use and abuse.[35] If this be so, it appears to reinforce my suspicions that God and substance abuse do not mix in much the same way as oil and vinegar. Cravings are at the heart of relapse and impede any meaningful participation by the addict in treatment (to include spiritually-based treatment). Cravings, and "urges" are at the heart of the substance relapse with the urge being the final state just prior to surrender to the craving for the drug of choice.

Gaining the participation of the substance abuser in the treatment setting is not a guarantee that positive results will be obtained. Laudet posited that 59.8% of those participants who enrolled in publicly-funded outpatient substance abuse treatment in New York City dropped out before they could complete the treatment program. Another 67.8% of those who dropped out did not provide any indication during surveys that a different approach for treatment would have ensured their completion.[36] In another reference to the study (Laudet), the participants of self-help groups such as NA stated they stopped attending because they were not interested in quitting their substance use habit in 31% of the cases. Further, in 25% of the cases, they felt they could quit on their own.

This trend of cessation of treatment affects all component parts of the treatment process. It includes the detoxification phase, when patients must be cleaned out from the toxicity from the substance and brought out of immediate health-related danger. It also affects initial treatment with a variety of inpatient treatment models such as AA's 12-step model, and post-treatment follow up through either a relapse prevention or AA 12-step strategy.

Once entering treatment, with the utilization of the AA 12-step model, the substance-abusing treatment participant is educated as to what amounts to spiritual principles. These principles are associated with turning one's life over to a higher power and believing that there is one who is greater who can resolve the addiction. (This occurs once the addict accepts the "truth" in the first step that they are powerless over the addiction). Fiorentine and Hillhouse reported that an "acknowledgement of loss of control over alcohol use predicted greater acceptance of the need for life-long abstinence."[37]

A transcendent experience is theorized as occurring during treatment and is further suggested to continue after treatment through AA participation.[38] Some of the individual AA steps that directly relate to an inquiry into spirituality are step two--came to believe that a power greater than ourselves could restore us to sanity; step three--made a decision to turn our will and our lives over to the care of God as we understood Him; step five-- admitted to God, to ourselves, and to another human being the exact nature of our wrongs; step six--were entirely ready to have God remove all these defects of character; step seven--humbly asked Him to remove our shortcomings; and step eleven--sought through prayer and meditation to improve our conscious contact with God as we understood Him, praying only for knowledge of His will for us and the power to carry that out.[39]

Of the 649 empirical articles on spirituality and substance abuse reviewed by one author for work with spirituality, there were 26 published articles suggesting that spiritual components, as a part of the treatment, helped the substance abuser.[40] In mentioning the phenomena of spirituality (associated with abstinence and successful treatment outcomes) present in empirically-based research, I used the keyword search of "abstinence" and "substance abuse." In many of the search results of the topic concerning these two key words, there is an association made between the topic and AA.

Vaillant associated AA participation with the development of spirituality and stated "men in the good outcome groups reported attending about 20 times as many AA meetings as the men in the poor outcome groups."[41] Miller stated that long-term abstinence rates for alcoholics who attended less than 100 meetings was at 20%, in contrast to a 53% abstinence rate for those who had attended more than 100 meetings of AA.[42] Brown et al. reported that the results of their research involving an intervention (as part of a 12-step AA recovery program), with the goal being to "know your higher power," resulted in a significant increase in spiritual involvement and beliefs over the pre-intervention period of 12 weeks earlier.[43]

Research indicates that populations in treatment who are actively involved in 12-step groups have higher rates of abstinence than those individuals who do not participate. Increased involvement is associated with improved treatment outcomes.[44] Being forced into treatment by pressure exerted from the legal system, employers, or family members does not lead to high rates of success towards abstinence as compared to active, voluntary involvement by the addict in AA. The AA meetings, activities, sponsorship, and 12-step work have been reported to result in greater success towards cessation of substance use and abuse.

Individuals who demonstrate dimensions associated with spirituality tend to experience a positive influence on their health (to include mental health) and research indicates that this influence operates as a "latent" variable.[45] According to Miller and Bogenschutz, "Adults and adolescents who are more religious are less likely to be using or dependent on alcohol or other drugs of abuse, both at the present time and in the future."[46]

Magura et al. stated that 12-step programs are successful due to the addict's perceived control over the addiction and sociability associated with these programs. (Spirituality is also a factor).[47] Neff and MacMasters argued that "spiritual transformation, at an individual level, takes place in a social context involving peer influence, role modeling, and social reinforcement"[48]. This has been theorized by the Social Model of treatment. These research efforts would suggest that spirituality is achieved through either a Social Model of treatment or through the Medical Model of treatment.

The medical model position is that addiction is the result of a personality disorder, primarily concerned with immaturity, primitive ego traits, and associated with numerous bio-physiological deficits, otherwise known as the disease concept of addiction. In a qualitative study by Redman, the utilization of spirituality to alter the abuse of substances was noted by over one-half of the participants. They provided comments (in reference to spirituality being associated with abstinence) such as, [spirituality] "restored their faith in God" [and] "recovery wasn't going to work without God and that God couldn't be an integral part of my life until I stopped using."[49]

McGovern et al. found that some individuals have encouraged the use of a holistic approach to drug treatment. This approach includes spirituality as but one component to that treatment.[50] It is important to encourage the development of strengths to overcome these immature and primitive vulnerabilities with the total person being considered. The strength of the inclusion of spirituality as a core component to treatment lies in the overall encompassing of the human experience that is found within spiritual lifestyles. As the attributes discussed with spirituality have suggested, most considerations for social, personal, and self-actualization issues are covered within the practice of this spiritual essence. Connor et al. supported the importance of spirituality over the long haul as recovery is enhanced with the presence of a spiritual belief system.[51]

Not all data supports spirituality as positive in the remediation of substance use, yet a caveat must be made to identify the entity that they define as being spiritual. Allen discussed that, in some cases, spirituality may lead to the individual determining what is moral, and experimentation may be an outgrowth of that spiritual experience.[52] In assessing this assertion, one must be careful to identify whether the individual is at the center of the experience or whether the individual is experiencing a relationship with a Creator. As my professional experience has indicated, those who are in a relationship, rather than being about themselves, do benefit immeasurably from the spirituality associated with recovery efforts.

Even though my professional experience has provided me with exposure to positive outcomes for those who have decided to seek and practice a spiritual lifestyle, there are some researchers who categorically refuse to acknowledge this. The group of researchers who refuse to accept the benefits of spirituality for recovery make up the minority view in my study of the available data. I question whether personal views have entered into their summary of the lack of benefits associated with spirituality. It is difficult to see how one group can see the benefit, while another refuses to endorse similar conclusions. This speaks to a diluting of the definition of spirituality,[53] the fallacies associated with the scientific method, and this potential personal signature on otherwise empirical research. Or, as Longshore et al. pointed out, the lack of clear means of pursuing research into religious and spiritual matters associated with recovery is a consideration.[54]

More often than not, the research results are promising for a positive correlation between religious or a spiritual experience and recovery from substance abuse. Granted, many of these individuals attend church and speak to the benefits that they receive from attendance. However, they state extensively that their personal walk with their Creator is at the core of their recovery. This walk has led to an experience that is described in the AA literature as a "spiritual awakening." It is a rare exception when recovering addicts who are experiencing the benefits of prolonged recovery do not refer to this awakening as a turning point to their recovery and a prime reason for their abstinence from substances of abuse.

In my research into the presence of spirituality as a precursor to abstinence and length of abstinence, I found many spiritual concepts were reported favorably by those who had a spiritual awakening and prolonged abstinence. Among them, the most prevalent included a belief that reading of religious texts and religious service participation were important to recovery (upwards of 50% +, that the respondents believed in God and that God was involved in their daily lives (all responded with "strongly agree" with exception of only one "disagree"). There was a mixed response regarding the idea that God would do things for them regardless of their behaviors. The question that "nothing that I do makes a difference because of God being so powerful" was the most divergently answered item of the SHI by the respondents.

Even though the respondents in my research had participated in a 12 step AA/NA recovery program, they did not agree with the program as to its importance as a means of achieving abstinence. Over 50% of those surveyed responded that they disagreed or strongly disagreed with the statement that AA/NA was important to recovery. A similar percentage also did not participate in AA/NA meetings or step work to include a sponsor. Further, about 35% stated that they attended AA/NA meetings and were abstinent while another 16% reported that they were not abstinent yet attended these meetings. This would suggest that the use of AA/NA is not totally convincing as a means of promoting an abstinent lifestyle universally, yet having a spiritual awakening is a more accurate barometer as to abstinence or extended recovery from substances of abuse.

Having a Spiritual Awakening

Lettieri, Sayers, and Pearson believed addiction can be resolved by a reliance on, and spiritual relationship with, a Higher Power.[55] In a study by Brown University, "The data suggest that people in recovery often undergo life altering transformations as a result of embracing a power higher than one's self … [that] leads to sustained abstinence."[56] One recovered addict referred to his transcendent experience as a "moment of clarity" in which he looked outside his window and saw nature that contrasted with the results of an alcoholic binge drinking episode inside his home. He stated that, "simple, but not easy; a price had to be paid.

It meant the destruction of self-centeredness. I must turn in all things to the Father of Light who presides over us all."[57]

Kaskutas et al. found that when a spiritual awakening was reported as a result of their AA involvement, individuals were nearly four times more likely to be abstinent three years post-treatment, than those who reported no spiritual awakening. In comparison, those individuals who had never reported an awakening accounted for 64% of those who failed to abstain.[58] As has already been stated in the introduction, in my research I found in all but one of the instances that the individuals who professed abstinence in recovery also stated that they had had a spiritual awakening as described in the question presented in the SHI.

A spiritual awakening is reported in research literature and popular print by any of a number of personalities from the field of music, movies, theatre, sports, and daytime television. Their portrayal of the experience usually follows the traditionalist experience of having an awareness of something greater than themselves that provides them with a knowledge or feeling of being in communion with a Creator.

My own awakening could well be defined in this manner and allowed me to understand things that I do not feel that I could, of my own intellect, have a clear understanding. The general sense that one has an understanding gained from a Creator's intervention into one's life. There is a knowledge of life that one finds as a revelation beyond one's own intellectual foundations and an awareness of the intricacies of our surroundings are just a few of the predominate feelings that are possible. These are some of what I can attest to within my own walk with a Creator. I have heard it stated by others many times that the spiritual awakening has occurred from being led to believe that God has a purpose for their lives. They felt that there is much more to their existence than what they have lived. For me, it was a knowing that came from a calm that overcame me and a peace of mind that surpasses what I could understand.

Munro found spirituality to provide "resolution" and "greater contentment in life" when the awakening occurs.[59] In her personal experience, the use of compact discs from accepted spirituality-oriented individuals was of importance, although the means by which one arrives at a spiritual awakening are as numerous as the people who experience them. In searching databases for material to present, as it related to spiritual awakenings, there were only a few instances when a "hit" occurred.

In my research into spiritual awakening, there were articles outlining the need for America to have a spiritual awakening as well as an article outlining an Indian experience with spiritual awakenings in the country as the result of a motorcycle accident and a subsequent shrine to the fallen cyclist. These search "hits" also included an article concerning the lack of God in Western civilization since the advent of the Industrial Age. It was theorized in that article that if had not been the case in the Asian continent since their industrial emphasis beginnings recently. However, there is little sharing of personal experiences of spiritual awakenings in research articles. Only instances of individual conversations with others in our lives allow us to appreciate the significance of spiritual awakenings and the powerful impact they have on the one experiencing them.

Chapter IV

Spirituality and Well-Being

～⚭～

Mental Health and Spirituality

Numerous authors have stated that spirituality is effective in improving psychological well-being,[60] mental health,[61] and quality of life.[62] Plante and Pardini reported that spirituality was associated with "increased coping, greater resilience to stress ... and lower levels of anxiety,"[63] further supporting the suggested advantages to spirituality. Within the parameters of Koenig's definition of spirituality—consisting of religious beliefs and behaviors, short of traditional participation and group associations—spirituality is responsible for multiple advantages and remediation from mental disorders and health issues.[64]

Furthermore, Koenig posited that lower levels of depression and quicker recovery from depressive episodes was related to spirituality. Reductions of the fear associated with anxiety, fewer suicides, and negative attitudes towards suicide are associated with "religious" (spiritual) patients.[65] The key to these lower levels of depression, fear/anxiety, and suicide include having the proper frame of mind or outlook on life.[66] In reference to the present economic downturn, Marques wrote that "a pessimistic outlook not only kindles anxiety which can put people at risk for chronic mental illnesses like depression, but may also cause early death. It (pessimistic outlook) can set people up for a number of physical ailments, ranging from the common cold to heart disease and immune disorders."[67] The work of both Koenig and Marques suggests that spirituality is important in the various domains of well-being.

In determining the extent or presence of anxiety and depression for those battling serious, advanced illness, an assessment of the individual's present spiritual well-being and past spiritual experience are important. Johnson et al. provided evidence that those with a past history of negative spiritual experience(s) were more apt to suffer from anxiety and depression when battling serious medical conditions. This was also considered true for those with a low present-day spiritual well-being status. [68] In comparison, those who possessed a strong spiritual state of well-being were less likely to suffer from anxiety or depression while seriously ill. This is theorized to be the result associated with having faith about the role of spirituality in dealing with illness and possessing a positive meaning, peace, and purpose to life. This faith serves as mediators of depression and anxiety and also serves to mitigate these mental states.

In their research on older adults' preferences for religion/spirituality approaches used within treatment for anxiety and depression, Stanley et al. found that older adults may be more religiously oriented than, say, younger adults or those battling terminal illness or chronic illnesses.[69] They go on to state that some religious and spiritual coping (e.g., church attendance) are positively associated with lower stress and depression levels, reduced rates of mortality, and other health-related benefits. In over 70% of those surveyed in their research, they preferred to have spiritual and religious themes addressed during mental health treatment. Finally, those that chose this addition of religious and spiritual themes were more likely to include God in their decision making for problem resolution.

In the book entitled, *How God Changes Your Brain: Breakthrough Findings from a Leading Neuroscientist*, authors Newburg and Waldman stated that thinking about God reduces stress, which leads to decreased deterioration of the brain's dendrites and increased neuroplasticity.[70] Further, permanent strengthening of neural functioning occurs with meditation and reflection on spiritual-related practices that assist in the reduction of anxiety and depression as spiritual practices positively affect those brain regions which serve as the origins for those disorders. My personal experience points to the absence of a spiritual connectedness when there is the presence of significant depression and anxiety for mental health clients seeking psychological services. In only a few instances do these individuals contemplate the impact of spirituality on the presence or absence of their distress and, when they do, they only theorize about God. Frequently, they have demonstrated little prior consideration of spiritual matters. Vasegh reported that those who do consider spirituality issues and concepts have improved mental health outcomes; recovering much quicker from distress associated with depression and anxiety, among other disorders.[71]

Schizophrenic patients who have expressed the self-importance of spirituality and religion were found to have more positive coping abilities to manage their schizophrenia.[72] Further attention to the subject of schizophrenics who professed a spiritual and religious interest led to the conclusion that less rumination on existential questions such as the meaning of life or of self-acceptance was found to occur for those patients, as compared to less spiritually- and religious-inclined schizophrenics. There have been opinions voiced that religious-oriented themes are associated with psychosis, but this has not been observed in the research associated with this work as personal religious beliefs do not equate with the presence of psychosis or delusions. It appears in secular-driven media to suggest that there is a lack of higher-level reasoning associated with spiritual-thinking for reaching decisions, yet I have not seen this to be the case in my work with clients or in private life.

At the chemical level within the brain, spirituality and practices associated with spirituality such as prayer and meditation were seen to be positive to optimal brain functioning for Buddhist monks and Franciscan nuns. Newberg and Waldman provided information that concluded that an increased blood flow to the frontal lobes and decreased blood flow in the superior parental cortice resulted from those activities.[73] This is to say that more activity occurs in the executive functioning area of the brain for the individual, while less physical representation of the self as a result from the meditative practices. As physical representation of self has to do with such aspects as compliance with social norms, a healthy, functioning individual is compliant, empathetic, and compassionate; over active physical representations result in rigidity, and hypo-activity results in apathy. Also, lower blood pressure and better immune functioning were reported as occurring for spirituality-oriented individuals.[74]

Physical Health and Spirituality

Stanton et al. reported a positive growth range (in spirituality) of between 60% to 95% as they relate to interpersonal relationships for those who had survived cancer—with a renewed sense of the value of self and others resulting from their brush with death in many instances.[75] These individuals also felt a change in goals and priorities, renewed sense of purpose, and placed greater importance on life. Stanton et al. stated that research indicates that those individuals who experience a post-traumatic state after suffering a significant trauma, grow spiritually.

It is theorized that those individuals who go through a traumatic medical event such as cancer are likely to engage in a spiritual or religious experience. This occurs concurrently to assist in dealing with the traumatic event. Denney, Aten, and Leavell reported that research participants who went through cancer treatments turned over their will to God and put their future in His hands. They reported a renewed trust and faith resultant from the surrender of control over their lives to the Creator.[76] Spiritual oriented messages from trained community health advisors about the need for testing to avoid cancer was also an example of the message to turn one's self over to a Creator for protection. In this instance it was to the spiritual community associated with a local church group.

Holt et al. reported that community health advisors used the principle of keeping the body clean as a temple for worship to impress upon church congregation members the need for colorectal cancer testing.[77] The results were modest, but indicate that important positive results occurred. Besides having an emphasis on colorectal cancer, many other health topics were provided to parishioners during a health fair as part of the overall program. This resulted in important implications for the use of spirituality as a means of the body temple.

In their research dealing with religion and spirituality in rehabilitation for traumatic brain injury victims, Waldron-Perrine et al. found that a number of health issues are positively affected by spirituality and religion.[78] They referred to works of various authors who indicate that religion and spirituality have a positive effect on

- Cancer
- Multiple sclerosis
- Spinal cord injury
- Rheumatoid arthritis
- HIV/AIDS
- Heart disease, and
- Diseases brought on by aging.

These researcher go on to propose that spirituality and religion have a positive effect on those suffering from Traumatic Brain Injury with better physical and mental health due to social support derived from the associations of believers.

Spiritual considerations and reflection or meditation on spiritual issues may actually increase for those who have been diagnosed with dementia, and access to spiritual resources is diminished for this group.[79] Carr et al. suggested that the little things, such as making efforts to understand and appreciate the patient, listening and attending to the patient, or showing compassion and a sense of connectedness were seen as very important. These "little things" were seen as spiritual, and resulted in a connectedness between caregiver and patient.

In research directed at Australian hospital patients by Hilbers et al., the results indicated that over 80% of those surveyed felt that spirituality had an impact on health.[80] Not only were the results indicative of spirituality having a positive effect, it could have a negative effect as well (theorized as being punishment or retribution for sin). Further, spirituality may lead to improved health habits that forestall the onset of disease or illness, as implied by the research indirectly. Besides spirituality and religious practices providing significant coping ability for people with medical problems ranging from arthritis, diabetes, and cancer. All of the suggested advantages of spirituality appear to be associated with improved coping skills for dealing with life issues in general.

Nichols and Hunt reported that for those suffering from chronic illness, the use of spirituality as a means of investigating the purpose of life for the sufferer is positive for coping with and management of the chronic illness.[81] Because they are potentially life-ending, chronic illnesses rob individuals of their certainty about life, thus it is important to consider those things that lead to control over and certainty of life experience. Reinventing or rediscovering the purpose of life is but one positive means of giving hope to those who all too often have little positive experience as a result of the illness.

In the perusal of the literature associated with the correlation between spirituality and physical health, it appears certain that the frame of mind of the individual who is attending to positive spiritual beliefs and thoughts leads to improved physical health. At a minimum, it is perceived to be so by the individual. The caveat here is to consider positive spiritual beliefs versus negative spiritual beliefs for improvements as evidenced by research undertaken by Rippentrop et al.[82] In that work it was stated that, "compromised mental health status was related to negative religious coping,"[83] such as being punished, abandoned, or avoided by the Creator. Those who felt that they were very spiritual (or religious) ranked better health-wise than those who did not self-report high levels of spirituality for themselves. A final point from Rippentrop et al. is that intense pain was associated with a lack of forgiveness and negative religious coping.

Faull et al. go so far as to suggest that the way that disability is perceived by the individual suffering with the infirmary may have an important impact on their health.[84] Those who utilize the "spiritual dimension of health" are prone to be less affected by the disability (or so it appeared to this writer when reading the material). Larson and Larson suggested a similar idea in their approach to spirituality's potential relevance to health when they reported that spirituality provided:[85]

- Improved coping skills,
- Enhanced pain management,
- Improved surgical outcomes, and
- Reduced risk of suicide.

In all of these instances the benefits seen from spirituality for improved physical health were resultant from the way people think or feel as a result of engaging in a spiritual lifestyle. Conversely, all Powell, Shahabi, and Thoresen were able to state with certainty was that those who were spiritual or religious lived longer.[86]

Chapter V

Current Trends Concerning Spirituality

~ ⦵ ~

The Direction and Diversity of Spirituality

A final area to consider in a discourse about the demise of spirituality is to assess the role of spirituality and how it is (or could be) marginalized (along with religion) by intellectuals within today's society. O'Connell and Skevington explained that there are other domains that some of the attributes that are associated with spirituality may also fall within, thereby excluding the domain of spirituality altogether from a discussion of quality of life.[87] These authors were discussing theoretical models associated with quality of life and determined that spirituality was a stand-alone domain that was important to a discussion of the quality of life of individuals.

Those attributes that were found to be associated with spirituality included spiritual connection, meaning to life, awe and wonder, wholeness, spiritual strength, inner peace, hope/optimism, and faith.[88] Further, O'Connell and Skevington stated that these qualities were, in some cases, capable of being closely associated with psychological or social domains of the person. As such it could be suggesting an "out" for those who choose to ignore or minimize spirituality as an integral portion of the quality of life of the individual. Instead, the idea is that these attributes could be cataloged differently. What appears possible to infer is that people have a social approach to life or place their connectedness or strength on social associations. This is apparent in man's interest in self and other human personalities for the majority of their daily existence at present. Thereby, they are missing the mark as to the spiritual basis of our existence with the relationship being between the practitioner and the Creator and Son.

This ignoring of spirituality in the traditional sense has already happened to a point, it is not a stretch to estimate that this trend will continue to occur, as evidenced by our history over the past 100+ years. Until the early 1900s, one went to a clergy member when there were critical issues and traumatic personal questions and this began to change with the origins of psychiatry and, later, psychology. Professional organizations, codes of ethics, and licensure requirements have been established for a full range of mental health professionals from social workers to marriage and family therapists to counselors and the already-mentioned psychologists and psychiatrists. HMOs and POS health care policies direct their consumers to these individuals in most all cases involving mental health issues, thereby suggesting that there is a clear demarcation between mental health and spirituality. This also is further suggesting that spirituality has little connection to mental health, much less the physical health, of their policy holders.

Traditional definitions of spirituality have changed and the interest has evolved to be more of a scientific and academic exercise versus a clergy-oriented search. This is readily apparent in an analysis of the trends associated with the articles presented on the relationships between religion, spirituality, and health. Weaver et al. reported that there had been a marked increase from 1965 to 2000 in the number of articles published regarding spirituality and religion/spirituality and its' connection with health. Meanwhile, those articles related to religion and health solely had decreased.[89] These authors thought that this may be due to spirituality being seen as subjective and transcendental, while religion is seen as an organized, formal means of worship that is falling out of favor.

Still another view is that this increase in spirituality interest in the research field can be categorized into various subheadings of material.[90] Analysis, education, and measurement serve as some of the ways spirituality is addressed, while other approaches include article reviews, the use of spirituality as an intervention, and its impact on communities. This would suggest that the concept of spirituality is being transformed to confine to scientific study and may be seen in a manner separate from what its actual identity consists of. The Vatican sees the embrace of spirituality as lacking the value of Christian faith, and therefore taking the concept of spirituality further toward that of science as well as farther away from the confines of having a faith origin is apparent to Catholic leadership via their statement in 2003.[91]

This trend is reinforcement for the idea that those who account for this pattern are less interested in religion and more interested in spirituality. As many of those involved in research are from academia or of an academic orientation, it stands to reason that the concept of increased education equals less faith is relative. At least this is my interpretation of my experience of working in the academic community over time as a student at various levels of educational pursuit. This does not mean that religion does not exist with all learned individuals, it merely reflects a trend to have increased educational attainment reliant on the scientific method and less interest in faith; personal or within professionally-reflected thought. Further, what constitutes spirituality is not based on a relationship with the Father and Son, instead, it is often a secular-oriented concept devoid of either entity.

We continue to become less and less traditionally spiritual as we evolve as a civilization, and in few areas, does this fact become more evident than with those who provide the mental health treatment. Only 21% of the American Psychological Association members polled claimed that religion was a very important part of their lives, while 48% claimed that religion was not really important to them. [92] This compares with 96% of the general American public that states that they believe in God along with 83% believing that they receive support from God in the Southern U.S. and Midwest U.S., 72% in eastern

U.S. receiving support, and 70% in the western U.S.[93] It seems that the more educated the individual the greater the propensity for loss of faith and increase in reliance on science and the scientific method. APA members surveyed were generally in agreement as to the importance of spirituality and religion matters, when asked to respond to a survey about the importance of the organization's publication of the periodical *Psychology of Religion and Spirituality*.[94]

The approach of researchers and modern-day care givers is to rely on the scientific method to explain anything or everything as it relates to the acceptable knowledge base. The obvious flaw to this assumption or modus operandi by these individuals is that right and wrong (as it relates to behavior) is not subject to a factual basis of numbers or experimentation. Further, neither is faith subject to the laws of science. There are infinite aspects to the human condition and experience that are outside the bounds of science to accurately or appropriately address what is relative, important, or in our best interests. This is seen as rigid, inflexible in some academic circles where science has, in fact, become the new faith and religion.

Science explains what God has developed and must necessarily make inventions based upon the availability of materials and compounds that were formed from a God that is infinitely more accomplished than anyone in science. Science allows the investigator to assume that they have some control over the subject or expertness as to the understanding of the element, condition, or situation when, in actuality, one moment's realization is quickly dashed by updates and revisions of another individual at a later time. In fact, much of science involves theories which, unfortunately, are given the status of being "facts" by a world hungry for the comfort of "knowing" that which is not known.

One author went so far as to suggest that medical staff professionals take the role of addressing spirituality where clergy is not readily available during critical care instances.[95] While the idea is well-intentioned, it does not seem plausible to expect much sound guidance to occur for the client in need of spiritual/religious-oriented attention. What is apparent is that those who may very well have little personal faith or spiritual lifestyle would be tasked to provide something that they may not practice in their own private lives. This could lead to the instance whereby having the needed support be unspiritual (or secular) without benefit of informed and experienced leadership to tackle sensitive, existential issues that someone in a life and death situation may want to discuss or consider.

Molzahn and Sheilds stated that approximately 3% of the bachelor level educated and around 6.9% of the master's and doctoral level educated nurses promoted spirituality as a part of the nursing role for themselves.[96] Further, up to 21.3% saw this topic as the purview of other professions and not something to be addressed by those in nursing. Thus, there is considerable conflict as to whom and when the topic of spirituality is to be addressed within the health care field. One study suggests that the medical staff engage the subject when clergy is not present, whereas the results of another study strongly indicated that spirituality issues are not an area of responsibility for them.

Windsor and Shorkey reported that, as a result of their research using the test measurement of the Christian Inventory of Spirituality, non-licensed staff who taught spirituality in a faith-based drug treatment program were responsible for a more spiritually-based program than were licensed staff members. The length of spiritual education was correlated with better results from treatment.[97] One can only hope that, with the inclusion of the topics of spirituality into educational programs for licensed professionals, this situation will improve. It seems relative to consider that those teaching the spirituality topics need be apart from a purely academically-based educational background to be truly effective in providing appropriate and useful attention to the topic of spirituality. Academia must understand its limitations and avoid attempting to tackle a topic that they are, by their very nature, ill-equipped to address.

While doing research to prepare this book, I was overwhelmed by the perverted departure from traditional ideas of spirituality that many intellectuals had chosen to write about in a few of the professional journals. Slife and Whoolery professed that the divergence between modern social science and religion/spirituality could be seen as science deals with objectivity whereas religion/spirituality deals with subjectivity. They continued that naturalism (inferred to be part of religion/spirituality) where there is not right versus wrong. They suggested a fallacy of faith due to it being associated with the unseen versus the scientific method.[98]

According to Slife and Whoolery, "naturalistist explain and interpret the objective world as if reference to God is irrelevant or superfluous"[99] and, in another sense, that God is immaterial. Speckhardt looks forward to the time when "the scientific method, with its basis in observation, analysis, and experimentation will be seen as the driving force for determining valid choices for public policy." [Further] "the word spirituality will slip from usage, since it's derived from something so debatable."[100] Sointo and Woodhead talked about a concept of selfhood, which was interpreted by this writer as the triumph of selfishness and self-centered over selflessness as a part of the holistic spirituality that supposes mind, body, and spirit as the goal of spirituality instead of having a meaningful personal relationship with a Creator.[101] Fundamentally, what is suggested is a basis of focus for self and humanity versus a focus on the created with the Creator.

On the other hand, a "flexible" means of functioning with the personality being disposed to have others' interests at heart is seen as beneficial to the individual—both the one with this flexible personality and to those who receive from its positive disposition.[102] Happiness that is arrived at through optimal functioning results when a spiritual orientation (i.e., a selfless manner of functioning) directs the actions of the individual and is seen as being different than the transitory happiness received from self-directed interests. As such, selflessness and otherness are seen as primary trait factors for those leading a truly spiritual lifestyle.

This selfhood is apparent in regards to the present generation reaching adulthood, as it is reported by Twenge and Campbell in their book entitled, *The Narcissism Epidemic*.[103] They reported that fully 10% of Americans in their 20s met criteria for narcissistic personality disorder and another 15% in that age group have narcissistic traits, thereby suggesting that approximately one out of every four Americans in their 20's is narcissistic. In answering a survey, 80% of adolescents in the 1980's answered that they "were important" as compared to 12% in the 1950's. This love of self is obvious to this writer in dealing with a generation that feels that they are often entitled absent obligations. It appears that some feel they are deserving of having their wants satisfied without much substantive effort or sacrifice provided to attain relative luxury and lavish lifestyles. This lifestyle is patterned after movie stars or athletes who make enormous amounts of money for pretending or playing a sport that earlier generations participated in predominately for the love of the game.

How does this relate to spirituality? What was once a selflessness of character and a desire to be a servant to others has become a drive to serve only oneself. It is a source of constant amazement when dealing with Americans in their 20's (and the teenage group) that it frequently is about themselves and not about any other relationships—spiritual or otherwise. It is important to note that 1 of every 4 does not represent the majority, lest one inaccurately condemn an entire generation. However, it is very compelling to see upwards of 25% of America's young adults falling into this statistical number.

The parameters of what constitutes spirituality have also evolved as cultures merge and ideas of one culture are introduced into another. Occidental influences find spirituality being a search for, and emersion into, the source of "energy" by the individual and becoming "one" with the universe. Spirituality that has a basis from religious teachings finds the individual attempting to become one with the Creator. This is in contradiction to the oriental emphasis on energy, or "chi." Still others seek, through prayer and meditation or contemplation, to reach a state of the wisdom of the ages as is the theme across many cultures.

Another divergent goal of spirituality is to leave the body and travel the cosmos as Tibetan monks were said to have been able to accomplish. This was accomplished while the Gordian knot kept the spiritual essence of the individual connected to the physical body that was in a semi-suspended state of awareness. Spirituality, in all of these modes, seeks to ease blood pressure and relax breathing, find an inward state that is impervious to daily activities, and reach a connectedness with a more transcending entity that escapes time, space, and circumstances; whether it be the universe, chi, or the Creator.

Although each of these themes appears separate and distinct, there is the overriding essence of supremacy in the form of the universe, chi, or the Creator. The central consideration involves making sense of these seemingly separate theorized origins from which we are apart and must reach out to become one with. Both chi and the universe fail the test of originality in this writer's estimation as they both have an origin from something else and do not appear tangibly of the beginning of time and space. In each of these cases, they have their origins from a Creator.

Only the Creator is of numerous cultural traditions, indicating a presence from the foundations of the earth and the universe. Many will argue and debate the likes of which would include the question of what came first—the chicken or the egg. I am certain that those who believe that the universe or chi is at the source of humanity would differ with my assertion. It stands to reason when some equate a stretching exercise routine and breathing/relaxation with being spiritual, then it follows that some will have issue with a spirituality of traditional mores involving a Creator.

Not only will there be disagreement there, in light of the present day departure from traditional spirituality (to a pagan/secular sense of spirituality within the past 20 years), the actual goals for the spiritual experience have drastically changed. One of the most disheartening statements that I have read concerning the state of a spiritual understanding of our world is found in the writing of Potts who stated that over a century ago, the universe was seen as alive and not viewed as "dead matter."[104] It appears that science has served to make philosophy so cold and calculating that we do not even have an awe of our world.

Spirituality versus Materialism and Hedonism

Spirituality consists of a practitioner and the Creator operating in unison. In order to understand spirituality, it is imperative to understand the means by which the individual comes to seek a spiritual experience versus seeking a non-spiritual experience. In understanding this choice of paths, it becomes possible to discern the divergence of the choices and how they serve as diametrically opposite extremes to human behavior. For the individual, the operation of personality towards the achievement of goals (individually and collectively) by basing their choices on their values is the beginning of understanding their path to a spiritual life. The identity of the individual serves to either pursue a spiritual course in one's lifestyle or, often times, to the secular-preferred opposite of hedonism.

Grouzet et al.[105] surveyed college students of 15 cultures and found that people operate primarily from intrinsic and extrinsic goals. These goals were stronger for those surveyed than pleasure pursuit (hedonism), or its opposite—self-transcendence (spirituality). However, in poorer countries, the individuals see financial success as less of a hedonistic measure (pleasure-seeking) and more of a security issue (fulfill needs for living) to provide for those they care for. The research further showed that spirituality was associated with conformity and community—two values that are highly prized in less hedonistic societies. And, as wealthier countries saw wealth, safety, and physical health more as a hedonistic consideration, it can be argued that the personal independence and self-indulgence are more prevalent in wealthier countries as opposed to conformity and community.

Schwartz found that in twenty countries surveyed, ten values were constant in all cultures of which hedonism made the list as one of the ten.[106] Schwartz further noted that as a value, spirituality was relative to some of the cultures, but not to others. On the other hand, religion was seen as a primary top ten value within these cultures. So the natural question to be asked is, "Why do some embrace the value of spiritualism while others embrace hedonism?" "What is the allure of hedonism?" In summary, religion is historically important to most all while spirituality is a practice that all do not prize. Further, those with luxury and wealth are seeing those resources as providing a pleasurable state, while the poorer individual sees the pursuit of these resources as a necessity and not a luxury.

Those intrinsic values previously referred to include self-acceptance, affiliation, physical health, and safety; whereas the extrinsic values alluded to include image, popularity, and financial success. Once a person has realized their intrinsic values, they are apt to be inclined to seek the extrinsic values as a primary goal. Saying it another way, intrinsic values were identified by Maslow as deficit needs for the most part while extrinsic needs are growth needs. The intrinsic values are needed for survival, while the extrinsic values make one feel good. It is this push to feel good (hedonism) that is appealing to those who already have satisfied their intrinsic value needs (have their survival more secure). My concern is that the belief in security of survival may be the very thing that leads to a lack of stability, sustainability, and continuation of civilization since we take our security for granted.

Those individuals in poorer countries have not experienced the luxury that is more prevalent in wealthier countries thus they are more need directed-it is a need that requires a reliance on others when they are unable to meet those needs. Historically, this has led to conquest in order to satisfy those unmet needs-those with the resources succumb to those lacking. This need is an initial basis for a relationship with the Creator; knowing that one is lacking and the help of an omnipotent one is required to provide for that need. So, ultimately the question becomes do I depend on a Creator or do I attempt conquest of others who have the resources that I desire? In contrast, the thought may occur when one is fulfilled: "Why do I need someone and for what do I need them? (This is hypothesized by this writer from personal observation.)

Materialism is the second head of the two-headed beast of hedonism and materialism which has plagued those who would prefer for a spiritual lifestyle to be advanced in Western culture. In its basest form, materialism is the act of having opulence or without lack to a point when excess begins to take over. It is not a question of having what is needed rather, materialism is having for the sake of having where a need does not exist. The fact with materialism is that, whatever you have it will not ultimately be enough; more will be desired. So, in summation of this beast, the desire to feel good and have more now take the place of being involved in a relationship with one who can provide what is needed; an obsession for possessions leaves many less-inclined to pursue a relationship with a Creator. The problem with this is that seeking hedonism and materialism directly will never result in existential success. Ultimately, emotional pleasure supersedes reason and rational-based behaviors.

Research indicates that the principle of consumption of goods is reduced by a spiritual lifestyle.[107] Specifically, spending for the sake of spending to present oneself as lavish and wealthy are not present with those who profess and demonstrate a spiritual lifestyle, in contrast to those without a spiritual lifestyle. In fact, spending on others versus self are seen as beneficial for old age with benefits such as, "peaceful, happy, calm and in better health in old age" from altruism prevalent in a spiritual lifestyle.[108]

Modern Themes versus Spirituality

Of the many attacks on traditional, conservative values in America, multiculturalism and diversity serve as being potentially profound impacts on the culture and spiritual basis of this country. Diversity and multiculturalism both present the need to appreciate all cultures within the country and not set one culture as supreme over the others. Multicultural ideals start with the premise that cultures are different, but not inferior, to one another. It continues that each cultural enclave should be taken in the context of the distinctive and unique individual beliefs and values of the culture, and not expected to conform to a national model. These movements seek to advance the idea that everything is permissible as long as it conforms to a specific culture—nothing is wrong and everyone is right—and this is the problem. This ideal denies the reality that we are all obligated to be obedient to a spiritual source and that those obligations are consistent across all cultures. Everyone can't be right, but different.

Viewing the multicultural issue from another spirituality standpoint involves looking at multiculturalism versus connectedness. A central spiritual theme is one of connectedness and whereas multiculturalism sees connectedness within the realm of culture as compared to a universal application throughout mankind. Collectivism as the opposite to multiculturalism provides a sacrifice of individualism for sameness (universality of humanity). It has been theorized that culture was viewed and studied according to the sameness of all peoples prior to the advent of the multiculturalism movement.[109] What we, as the sum of humankind, had in common or what comprised our sameness was at the root of the cultural inquiry. In short, the connectedness of culture across the various component parts that make up the whole was at the focus of the study. Now, being different is "in" culturally, just as individualism is chic also in common present-day society.

Now, aspects concerning culture are viewed as they relate to the component parts rather than the sum total of (universality) humankind. Summarily, connectedness is seen as the mesh within culture rather than that which unites humankind. And, the real threat is in the development of an "us" and "them" mentality, rather than seeing mankind in the same boat with those issues plaguing some as a threat to all. This results in a general lack of connectedness; that which is at the heart of a spiritual existence of collectivism. Having the same biological, physiological, and organic structure is overlooked for a perspective which represents a single portion of the overall human. A lack of rational consideration of the situation is a root cause for this conflict of culture versus our human connectedness.

Sandage and Harden found that differentiation of self, religiously related personal quests, and gratitude were positively associated with intercultural development and that spirituality grandiosity was negatively correlated with intercultural development.[110] In short, having a genuine love for humanity and self-satisfaction with one's state spiritually is seen as a positive contributor to connectedness. Seeing self as a culture apart from our mutual identity breads disinterest and division between cultures. These researchers went on to state that those who were drawn to religious programs may be unwilling to develop inter-culturally, while those who used their spirituality to support self-felt importance or preeminence culturally are not disposed to intercultural development. What may be missing in Sandage and Harden's research is the factor that multiculturalism that focuses on the development of between-culture acknowledgements and acceptances may be ill-equipped to address the need of individuals to be viewed and considered as a collective of humankind. This is as compared to being disjointed and indirectly marginalized into the otherness (individuation) found in a multicultural study of humanness.

Spiritual lifestyles are based on the premise that there is a Creator who has specific expectations for us in order to exist in a relationship spiritually. It stands to reason that one person's Creator does not think differently than another person's Creator. In a spiritual relationship, there are absolutes and this is where the issue is for multiculturalism and diversity. Some say that anything goes as long as it conforms to a culture; spirituality says that there are absolutes that transcend culture.

On the surface, it appears safe to say that all cultures have certain absolutes such as the prohibition against murder, although life does not hold the same sanctity in all cultures.

Rape is seen as inappropriate although it has been reported that approximately 70% of the world's female population experiences abuse of some type during their lifetimes. The actual role of females in society based on culture is divergent, thus the lack of a spiritual universality exists there. To deny that there are absolutes of conduct that are universal in nature is to support multiculturalism and diversity where variety is encouraged and supported. Its very existence is a refutation to traditional spirituality that professes a universal adherence to a Creator.

In her argument for a proper and effective means of the study of culture, Cauce gave a rundown of the evolution of science as it has arrived to the present time.[111] Within this discussion was the development and evolution of psychology as a science and how it led to multiculturalism. The suggestion or inference made was that the practical, procedural methodology of science was able to determine the essence of human existence within the field of psychology. Further, multiculturalism was able to accomplish this within the area of culture. The unpredictability of humankind serves to make this argument inaccurate as the quest for absolutes of humankind fall short within scientific study. Only an assessment of conduct towards the adherence to absolutes taken from an existential standpoint is sufficient to understand humankind I suppose. A spiritual examination lends more accurate and enlightening information that any amount of scientific method utility for understanding the connectedness of humanity. Our spiritual roots are such that attempts to mitigate our identity through any science is artificial and shallow in an understanding of our souls.

Spirituality Possession and Behavioral Issues

The concept of spiritual intelligence is viewed by some authors as an "ability to solve problems that relate to values, vision and meaning" and creativity is a chief component of that intelligence.[112] Other writers have said that spiritual intelligence also involves the "capacity to be virtuous," and "expressed in the world through wisdom, compassion, and action."[113] What is common to this concept is the predisposition to look at situations or problems with a view of how the Creator would view them. We commonly ask what the Creator would do in a particular situation and devise a strategy accordingly. It is theorized that this spiritual intelligence is developed and serves as one of the prime components of the overall intelligence of humankind.

It stands to reasons that those who possess a spiritual basis to their personality have developed this division of overall intelligence to a more advanced state than those who do not understand, appreciate, or adhere to a spiritual lifestyle. Further, failure to adhere to a spiritual lifestyle, on the societal level, leads to the decay in the fabric of that society. When one sees the "it is all about me" mentality prevalent with the up and coming generations, it is not a stretch to envision how this potential loss of a component of overall intelligence may occur. If it truly is all about oneself, then there is no room for being subservient to another, thus no relationship can exist between the created and the Creator. What may be gained with the advent of the computer (and the infinite information available with the Internet) will be far overshadowed by what is lost in individual ability to reason. Scripture states that we will forever seek knowledge but fail to come to the truth. This example provides the basis for a lack of confidence in the information age to satisfy our spiritual existence. It certainly does not provide for our sustainability when the soul is considered. Nor does it allow one to think in a manner that includes virtue and wisdom, courage to do things that may not be popular, and follow one's conscious. The scientific method has its place, but it is not all encompassing. Spiritual intelligence is necessary to address social issues that number crunching cannot resolve. Our ability to live in peace with each other and in response to our obligations to each other (and to our Source) and does not find form in science.

Wink and Dillon state it succinctly when they say that "the association between spirituality and wisdom means that highly spiritual individuals display a complex way of thinking and possess insight into the human condition."[114] This statement serves to epitomize the distinction between those who do not operate on a spiritual basis and those who do as it relates to behavioral issues. Those without the benefit of a spiritual lifestyle are impervious to many issues involved in the discussion of right or wrong (morality-based arguments). They do not demonstrate the understanding of the complexity found with a spiritual-based consideration in approaching living life.

Chapter VI

The State of
Spirituality in America

Church Attendance and the State of
Spiritual Education

Zinnbauer, Pargament, and Scott prepared a comprehensive statement concerning the state of spirituality and religion with some rather dubious statistics made available by them as well (as other contributors) that are worthy of note:[115]

- Except for the instances of the phenomena of conservatism, church membership has deteriorated significantly since the 1940s with some religious denominations (Episcopal and Methodist churches were cited) losing more than 35% of their memberships in a span of around 30 years."
- Between the 1960s and 1970s, approximately 60% of baby boomers had left organized religious involvement for two or more years.

- Spirituality expanded its base and following in the 1980s and 1990s with spiritual organizations numbering over 400 by the 1980s.
- Many of these new spiritual groups are not spiritual in the traditional sense of following or searching for a Creator.
- It is estimated that as much as 72% of 18- to 29-year-olds have adopted the descriptive explanation for their faith as "spiritual but not religious" as is also the case for up to half of the non-church individuals.[116]

What appears relative for these "new" forms of spirituality is that they do not require a subservient position to a Creator by the practitioner. Reality is that they can be all about themselves. This is while they search for something to fill the void left by a lack of belief in the tenet of a traditionally-organized faith. Where there is adherence to a traditional form of Judeo-Christian or Muslim faiths, many times it is of the conservative and uncompromising type that allows for no divergence from the standards set in place by, in many instances, charismatic leaders. What is left is a division of people into two camps from the opposite extremes of the spectrum. In short, there is no middle ground for these groups to meet (evangelical versus secular) in a balanced form.

The idea of love being the guiding force of Christianity is misrepresented by secular-oriented society that sees it as a means to avoid compliance with scripture. For the radical Islamist, the principle is seen as a sign of weakness as they attempt to conquer to forward their faith. It appears to be a basic assault on long-standing, traditional attempts at promoting Christian doctrine in the world. This is due to the fact that seculars find evangelicals as "harsh" and seemingly rigid without the love that they rely on to avoid compliance as a requirement for spiritual lifestyles. This scenario has placed the world in conflict with division being more common than finding agreement and shared worship of a like, spiritual nature.

This dichotomous difference is discussed by Straughn and Feld as a byproduct of the claim by many in America that we are a "Christian nation."[117] It appears that the more we diversify as a nation religiously, the more some components of the nation see us as being a religious nation-as high as 71% in 2005). This belief by religious peoples of the United States being a religious nation at the exclusion of those who do not actively practice a faith leads to increased potential hostility. This is the interpretation that this writer has gained from the research and spiritual experience that serves as a basis for this work. And this increased potential for hostility is at the core of a division within the country between religious, spiritual, and secular population segments in America. This division could serve to splinter the national consensus in the United States on a number of issues that are based on religious versus secular stances. We continue to see this happening with secular-based positions alienating and marginalizing those religious and spiritual portions of the population. Their beliefs are being systematically expunged from the legal codes with social turmoil only being guaranteed by their implementations.

Although Zinnbauer et al. found that, in spirituality, there are standards that are based on traditional religious standards in 63% of the time, spirituality allows for a lack of obedience or adherence to a representative of religious affiliations. In fact, the source of spiritual discernment with a proxy guiding the discovery may be fulfilled by mental health and medical professionals who are just beginning to have spirituality addressed within their training curriculums. Having recognized the importance of spirituality in well-being, doctors, social workers, and psychologists are including an attention to issues associated with spirituality.

The Chronicle of Higher Education, a journal devoted to issues with education, indicated that this is indeed the case for social workers and medical professionals. In an article dated March 7th, 1997, the Chronicle reported that medical schools begin teaching spiritual side of medical care with reference to Loyola's chaplain-mentor program for medical students.[118] In the May 18[119], 2001 issue of the Chronicle, reference is made to the University of Kansas and the Society for Spirituality in Social Work founded in 1989 and that over fifty accredited programs in social work now offer coursework in spirituality.[120] The importance of the affirmation of life's purpose and meaning to life in times of grief and loss are but one instance when spiritual issues are relevant in these fields when working with clients. Not advancing specific religious dogma while being attentive to the needs of a suffering client requires this approach.

In the field of psychiatry and in professional counseling, professional accreditation agencies are ensuring that the topic of spirituality is receiving attention. Spirituality is being seen as an important aspect to address in treatment for clients. Dein pointed out that the Accreditation Council for Graduate Medical Education requires clinical instructions in religion and spirituality to account for a portion of the training in psychiatric care component during psychiatrist training.[121] Nichols and Hunt referred to accreditation standards for counseling education programs to include competencies associated with spirituality as a part of the curriculum of professional counseling.[122]

Various Segments of the Population and Spirituality

In a study of rural, low-income female heads of household, the greatest single contributors to wellness was having a spiritual, purpose-filled life. In the study of spirituality and religion versus wellness, the Purpose in Life subscale and the Private Religions Practices subscale of the conducted survey supported these findings. Both spirituality and religion were found to be significantly related to wellness in all subscales of these test domains. They were highly predictive of wellness (race/ethnicity did not matter), with all races or ethnicities being affected by spirituality and religion as to the level of, and the extent of, wellness. All told, 38% of the accounting for wellness could be traced to spirituality and religious emphasis in Gill, Minton, and Myers' research.[123]

Adolescents have also been found to benefit from religious involvements (spirituality as well). The hopelessness that may be present in the adolescent's life is mitigated by religious participation and a spiritual lifestyle. Chang-Ho, Perry, and Clarke-Pine reported that drug and alcohol abuse and non-drug related crimes were less likely to occur with youths who participate in religious activities. These activities included "the practice of a religion that is internalized, cognitively oriented, and treated by individuals as a way of communicating with God."[124] They further discussed that suicide and depression for teenagers were less likely with increased religious involvement. This appears to be because the practice of religion is a means of positively dealing with negative stressors such as suicide ideation, depression, or anxiety.

University of Missouri research indicated that youths associated spirituality with positive behaviors such as having "self-confidence … conviction … impetus for virtue … connectedness … purpose … [and a] … foundation for well-being."[125] Having these behaviors appears to lead youth away from risky behaviors that could be destructive for them. Further, they suggest the spirituality-related positive behavior lead to the inception of growth and personal awareness. This, in turn, leads to spiritual connectedness and prosocial lifestyles.

Spirituality in children (up to the ages of 12) was the subject of research by Holder, Coleman, and Wallace as well as Ruddock and Cameron.[126] In Holder et al., the primary focus was to determine the relationship between spirituality and happiness, and they reported that between 3% and 26% of the child's happiness was linked directly to their measures of spirituality from the survey (not religious participation). Children's positive personal interpretation of personal worth and meaning to their lives as well as community connectedness were indicators of elevated levels of spirituality. Further, girls scored higher on the happiness scales than boys did, and public school students scored higher than did private school students.

In Ruddock and Cameron's research, so vividly and eloquently introduced, the emphasis was on measuring the spirituality of children and hypothesizing about its existence and extent. They noted that the spirituality of a child (up to ten years of age on average) involves the development of a morality with values, beliefs, and principles directly derived from spiritual self-inquiry and personal reflections. Those children who experience spirituality develop an awareness and understanding of their own and other's beliefs. They cultivated a respect for themselves and for others and developed a sense of empathy with others. This is seen in concern and compassion [and] an increasing ability to reflect and learn from this reflection.[127] This is supportive of my treatment of the topic of spiritual intelligence and of the sensitive period for development of it during this age group. A foundation of understanding regarding spiritual principles during this timeframe will serve the individual throughout their life. As such, it will be invaluable to positive mental health to deal with challenges relating to the entire life developmental model of living. As was indirectly suggested within the article, spirituality allows one to come to terms with life and accept what is presented which is a major lesson in the life of a child.

Unfortunately, it appears that there is a significant drop in the spiritual and religious development for adolescents who are ending their secondary school education. Good et al. discovered that this was the case between the 11th and 12th grades for those adolescents who were studied to determine the course of development spiritually/religiously.[128] This work indicated that religious activity involvement, prayer, meditation, and wondering all decreased significantly between those two final years of high school education. Further, Hardy added to this discussion with the findings that warmth from parents was positively associated with religious involvement for adolescents entering adulthood. No other parenting styles were significant predictors of future involvement by college-age, young adults.[129]

Regarding college-age students, a study by Fife et al. indicated that black college students who were "highly religious" were less likely to drink alcohol, have risky sexual behaviors, and more likely to exercise.[130] They reported that spirituality had a negative connection with alcohol use and problems. Also, spirituality was negatively associated with depression, anxiety, and sexually promiscuous behaviors. And, even though a lower percentage of college students ascribed to a relationship with God than the general population, over 70% stated that God was important in their lives and they believed in God.

From a standpoint of family resilience, families are best able to be successful if they have a shared belief system where "a positive outlook in life, a strong sense of purpose, and high levels of personal efficacy."[131] An internal locus of control (their fate was in their hands, rather than in another's) was also associated with successfully overcoming family challenges. Both of these sets of items underscore a very strong sense of spirituality. This was found to be present as a source of coping skills available to face adversity. The importance of spirituality was said to be crucial in being successful in overcoming things that stood in the way of the family's success.

From the community standpoint, the emphasis of spirituality has gained momentum over the past decades to be featured at conferences in 1997 and 1999.[132] It was stated by Maton that spirituality assists the individual and community in areas of coping, human diversity, socialization, and empowering.[133] It was considered worthy of note by Maton that the number of articles associated with the topic that were included in the Journal of Community Psychology equated with a total number ever published in the collective past of that journal. His estimation was that spirituality was beginning to get the recognition of which it was deserving.

A note of qualification involving cultural differentiation on the subject of spirituality was made by Fischer et al., who stated that in the Muslim world, the practice of a spiritual lifestyle was of the intrapersonal means versus Christian interpersonal means of practice.[133] What was purported was that Muslim world practitioners were more dependent on group support for their spirituality practice. This was in comparison to the individualism of practice by Christian spiritualists. Whether or not this theory is entirely true is open to discussion as the individual questions and ponders this claim.

Not only are their suppositions of otherness to spiritual practices separate and distinct from Western spirituality, the actual purpose to spirituality is distinctly different in Japanese culture. They have less than 10% of the population associated with an organized religion.[134] Roerner found Japanese were interested in the well-being aspects of the person—both of the living as well as of the dead ancestors. Theirs is a physical, rather than a cognitive, exercise of practice. They commonly have shrines in homes and, in Buddhist temples, they characterize the active practice of their spiritual lifestyles. And, Japanese are apt to turn to spiritual support in times of trouble.

The Meaning and Purpose of Life

Perhaps the greatest single quest that is undergone with a spiritual existence is the quest to find meaning and/or purpose to life. This quest has been embarked on, it can be theorized, by humankind since before recorded history. Many of the greatest personalities that have inhabited the planet have written on the subject. King Solomon, considered one of the wisest individuals to have ever lived, stated in the Book of Wisdom that the purpose of life was to serve God. This belief was arrived at after having experienced a wide gamut of situations within his own life. Victor Frankl wrote a seminal work entitled, *Man's Search for Meaning*, which has been reprinted countless times and is a favorite book on many bookshelves.[135]

As previously discussed, the purpose of life and the meaning to life are at the core of many individuals' spiritual experiences. At one time or another it is safe to assume that most all of us have considered these questions. Marston, in her research on baby boomers and their perceptions of the meaning of life, found that a connectedness with a significant other, with God, and with nature are at the core of the spiritual meaning of life. This list was arrived at according to the self-report of those participants surveyed.[136] Personal experience has provided this author with the benefits of having had positive personal experiences to these connections, although many of those clients with whom I work have a general lacking in regards to connectedness which significantly contributes to their psychopathological symptoms. It is safe to say that there are parts to this connectedness that are often missing. In therapy, this is the common acknowledgement in response to considering their connections to family, community, and Creator when they will respond.

Social well-being has been associated positively with connectedness to the social fabric of which the person is a part or so it is stated by Yoon et al.[137] In both the instances of connectedness (within-ethnic and other-ethnic), the concept of social well-being in association with acculturation is mediated by connectedness. In short, when one is entering into another cultural system the ability to be in positive association is essential to positive growth. However, just where the individual comes into play for this connectedness is open to debate, according to the works by various researchers. Mauss et al. found that the happiness shown by the individual toward others serves as an enhancing signal that allows for the development of connectedness between that person and others.[138] They theorized that the emotional behaviors must be genuine and lead to positive psychological functioning to allow for the development of improved connectedness. Also, depressive states are more prevalent when social connectedness is lacking.

Gray et al. theorized that sadness may increase the need or desire for social connectedness.[139] Individuals who are sad attend to cues of emotion and are apt to be motivated to seek out connectedness. It appears that emotional expression lends itself to a greater sensitivity to the emotional wiring of others. Certainly connectedness has specific positive benefits that are among the most beneficial; a safety against substance abuse and suicide as it was determined in a study of Alaskan native youths by Mohatt et al. In that study, connectedness encompassed the interactions between the youth as their families, community, and natural environment.[140] These are primary components of a spiritual connectedness and more research would be helpful to ascribe the benefits of connectedness to these components of individual existence.

De Klerk, Boshoff, and Van Wyk associated the purpose of life in connection with the work place and found that work motivation and career commitment at the work site are associated with meaning in life.[141] Specifically, these researchers indicated that spiritual level has a direct bearing on "goal orientation [and] intrinsic motivation." There was a distinct, positive correlation between the two.[142] The more successfully established the meaning to life, the higher the motivation at work appears to be what was suggested by their research. Thus, it appears appropriate to view finding the purpose of life and the meaning to life as related to achieving practically all aspects of life's benefits. This supports the idea that when one likes the work they do they typically perform better and more effectively in their work activities.

A sentinel event in the development of my own understanding of the purpose of life and meaning to life was uncovered while reading a segment of Frankl's book. He referred to the fact that although the Nazis had control over him and his life, they were not responsible for his attitude. It was entirely within his purview to control how and in what manner he would act in spite of the overwhelming misery inflicted upon him by his captors.[143] Although a small part of the journey, this passage forwards the reality that we are the captain of our own vessel in life and it is within our ability to succeed.

Chapter VII

My Spiritual Manifesto

A predominant reason for this work was to positively affect those who read it. My intention is to support the idea that God matters, in much the same way as I determined such to be the case as a very young adolescent in the 1970s. Whether this has indeed been the case, I cannot fully know. However, the evidence is compelling to come to a conclusion that having a spiritual relationship with a Creator is at least worthwhile, if not to be preferred. If it is to be for the overall, general benefit of having improved coping skills to handle everyday stress or overwhelming events that tax the strength of the individual, then that should be sufficient to encourage development of that relationship. If some are primarily interested in having a purpose to their existence, then this relationship is relative to a discovery as to why they are here. And, should the person be guided by a desire to have physical or mental health well-being, then a spiritual experience is mandated to achieve the maximum benefits of this well-being.

When working with clients in the mental health field, I find that the pleasure principle of Sigmund Freud is relative to dealing with their issues. Almost universally, they are concerned with achieving a pleasurable state while avoiding pain and anxiety. In short, they want to be happy. Being happy is not always about having something, but rather about coming to an acceptance of what they already have as being enough. This is where a spiritual relationship is paramount. One knows that one is but a small cog in the wheel, and that God knows what one needs. He will supply those needs. Nothing else is really needed; no other ingredients are necessary. That is at the beginning of the development of a relationship with a Creator that recognizes the place of both parties. Further knowing the benefits to having the relationship as well as knowing where there is an obligation to allow the Creator to be sovereign is essential.

The paradox of happiness is described as looking elsewhere, seeking to make a difference in the world and, in so doing, finding happiness as a by-product of our efforts. This is arrived at by leading a moral, decent life that is a credit to society rather than being a burden.[144] Martin referred to a subjective well-being or happiness that was not of the philosophical "true" type that means pursuit of a higher ground approach to all of life's challenges. In one sense, happiness is discovered on the community level by having a social connection that includes a connection to the location of the individual.[145] Leyden, Goldberg, and Michelbach found that the connection to the place where the person lives as important. The availability of the location for use by the community allows for a pleasurable state by the inhabitants.[146] I am not referring to the community basis; however, the individual is at the focus of and purpose of the treatment of the topic of happiness. I state that it is derived from a spiritual state of being that does not seek it, but finds it as a byproduct of other efforts.

Happiness is not discovered by looking for it, but by looking elsewhere and failing to ponder its existence. Martin referred to many principles of life, not the least of which was hedonism (seeking pleasure for pleasure's sake) which he stated served to cheapening life by the pure pursuit of pleasure. Instead, pleasure was seen as a derivative of happiness brought to bear by observing moral standards from spiritual living. Leading a moral, decent life is not about adoring artists or athletes, politicians or explorers, or leaders in various fields, nor does it optimally involve the meditation of the tranquility of a setting apart from the Creator's impact on that setting. Happiness is enjoyed in many ways, but my experience has been such that happiness is best served in a melding of oneself with that which brought us into existence. After all, he is from whom we were formed. In the spiritual sense, happiness comes from an awareness of and compliance to that for which we were made. It is both a natural and sensual experience from the act of living in obedience to our Creator.

In a pursuit of happiness or hedonistic pleasure derived from happiness, some of the following principles are relative to a spiritual existence in everyday life (thus moral, decent existence):

- Do not go into situations with expectations. If you have an expectation you can be disappointed, frustrated, angry, disillusioned, or distressed just as well as being satisfied. Your odds at being happy and content, even at their best, are only 50/50.
- On the other hand, having no expectations sets one up to be pleasantly surprised and if things do not happen as one would like, one is only occasionally disappointed.
- Do not be happy because something happens, be happy in spite of something occurring. If something must happen in order to be happy then you may or you may not be happy. If you are happy in spite of something happening, then you will be happy most of the time; or at least, more often happy than not.
- Do not be happy when you get to a place, be happy during the journey toward that place. More is learned and experienced on the way than just arriving there.
- Everything happens for a reason; we are not able to understand it, but that does not mean that it was not meant to be—just that we are not as wise as our Creator.
- If your aim is to acquire possessions, you will always want more. You can never acquire enough possessions to satisfy an appetite that craves goods.
- The person who forgives—not necessarily the one being forgiven—reaps the reward of improved mood and functioning.
- God is unable to forgive those who fail to be forgiving to others.
- Only the Creator has the right to judge anyone—our only obligation to others is to love them unconditionally.
- Everyone is of equal value; in spite of what we may think of someone, it is the Creator's prerogative—not ours—to determine

the value of the creation. Therefore, do not seek out those of means at the expense of those who may be downtrodden; do your best for all humankind.

- No one "makes" us do anything. In spite of the possibility that our choices are limited or appear distasteful, we always have a choice to do something or not do it as long as it does not affect us or others adversely.

All of these concepts are designed to allow the individual to have the greatest opportunity to achieve a pleasurable state. This allows for avoiding the pain and anxiety of taking control of our own lives instead of giving up control to a Creator who is infinitely better equipped to plot our course through the rough seas of living. That is the second lesson of development of a spiritual relationship with God-give up control because we will only screw it up. Being human means that we do not have the answers to problems with the consistency necessary to be able to be effectively in charge of our lives. We have a significant risk of error—God is required.

Now that you have turned over your cares to the Creator and have acknowledged the rights and responsibilities of that relationship, you can begin to explore the reason for your existence. There will always be those with and those without. Those without need our help versus those with who do not have need of help. We were placed on this planet to help others rather than to be self-serving and that is the primary reason for our existence. The two points to remember about this experience of finding our purpose are

- When our time on Earth is over, the only thing that we will have is what we have given away to others.
- No matter what we give away; if we do give away, we will end up receiving much more than we could possibly give away.

My experience has been that God knows what we need before we know it, including how much we require, and when it has to be there. The biggest challenge to this step of the spiritual journey is to realize that what we need, we will receive in God's time. It will not be on our schedule. Again, He is infinitely wiser than we are able to comprehend, and reflection is able to provide us with the insight that He was right on time—even when it did not seem so at that moment.

Once these steps have occurred, one can get down to a day-to-day relationship with its ups and downs and grow in the love and closeness that any interpersonal relationship has as its hallmark. There will be times that we will forget and try to take charge of a situation. Hopefully, we will learn the lesson without too harsh a penalty for our misguided feelings of competency. We are not "all that," as the younger generation says. The key factors as we go through the relationship at this juncture are

- God is not interested in where you have been. He is interested in where you are going. The relationship is for the strong of heart that will have faith until the end and not falter somewhere short of the finish line. We need to always be growing in our relationship.
- We, as parents or guardians, do not give our children everything that they want, but we do supply their needs. Occasionally, we provide what they want. God is no different in His relationship with us, His children. Be careful what you ask for-you may get it.
- If we are in an intimate relationship here on earth, we want our partners to put us first in their lives with their loyalty and allegiance to us instead of others. This does not change with God when we enter a relationship with Him.
- If we truly have faith and accept that God is who He says that He is, and is capable of what He says that He can do, then we will not doubt Him. It can be no small insult to lose faith in someone in whom we have entrusted our livelihood and being to. If things do not turn out like we want or how we believe that they should we must keep faith in his wisdom. No relationship is able to withstand tests without faith.

Having a spiritual relationship with a Creator takes communication. I ask clients who engage me in a spiritual conversation how much time they spend talking to people each day. Although these people may, in some cases, be able to lighten the load of the client, how much do these people provide in the way of support to them? The answer is that they do not provide any support for the most part. In comparison, how much support can my clients expect to receive from a Creator? The answer is obvious, and so communication is the key. If we would spend even one-fifth as much time talking in prayer to a Creator as we do to our acquaintances, neighbors, friends, and coworkers each day, we would be investing a great deal of time sowing for a harvest at some future point. I do not expect "pennies from heaven," but I can attest to numerous times when prayers were answered with a financial windfall in my life and my debts were erased.

This ability to be able to receive provisions that allow for our comfort does not come without a cost. Although we may benefit from having no lack by being satisfied with what we have and receiving what we need, we need be aware of the adage:

- To those that receive, they must return the harvest to the less fortunate, or as it is written (paraphrased), for much is received then much will be required in return to others. A true testament to faith is to be able to walk with the Creator by doing what has been modeled for your own life by that Creator. If He has provided for you, then it stands to reason that the proof of following where the Creator leads requires giving to others as has been done for us.

Does spirituality matter? Tovar-Murray conducted a study to determine the association between variables of religion and spirituality, and found that it does matter.[147] Religious participation/behaviors and spiritual beliefs are related to happiness, marital satisfaction, and health (both physical and mental). This research indicated that increased health and well-being are the results of the variables of religious behaviors and spiritual beliefs for those who were worshipers of a God. They benefiting from their faith and the practice of that faith. Walsh reported that people who practice religious or spiritual principles live, on average, seven years longer than those who do not. Further, it was reported that over 90% of the world's population engage in some form of religion or spiritual practices.[148]

It seems pointless to continue to advance the concept of spirituality for physical and mental well-being beyond that which has already been exposed through this treatment of the subject. It appears obvious that this is a journey that some will not embrace while others will. Those that do will reap a reward in multiples beyond their initial expectations or hopes, and be exposed to a fullness to their existence that they cannot find from any other source. The peace of mind and stability to one's person that a spiritual lifestyle allows cannot be measured or valued by common methods. It transcends that which one is able to describe. All I know is that it works.

Chapter VIII

Facing Reality and Our Source

I have purposefully left unmentioned in any great detail, scriptural or religious-related, spiritual passages within this book. In most instances this was done for the same reason that Christ stated that he came to attend to the ill. His inference was that those who were "well" were not in need of active intervention. Since many claim to be turned off by God's inspired words, I try to meet them where they are. However, some scriptural knowledge is required so that they may even begin to grasp what is at stake. Further, scripture states that one must first be given "milk for babes" so as to, in effect, understand the rudimentary ideals and basic information before tackling heavy, or deep, passages with multiple (somewhat subtle) things to consider. The idea is that I am attempting to fundamentally "plant seeds" with the hope that there are those who will feel led to further investigate and develop their own relationship with the Father and the Son. The problem with this lack of insight being offered is that I feel that I have not responsibly attended to those who are "lost" (as scripture states that I should).

This may seem to be a feeling that is not understood by the reader. In order to understand this they only need consider a few passages of scripture to be aware of the urgency to my concerns. In the final pages of scripture it is stated that, at the moment just before the return of the Son, the entire universe will be "silent and still." This may seem like a rather minor detail until someone considers the full effect of this statement. The enormity of the universe, and that its' being totally still and silent seems literally impossible-yet scripture is clear. The incredible nature of this passage need be fully appreciated so as to understand further the gravity and extent for my concerns. Consider further.

The idea is that there is, upon this return, a "judgment seat" that all will pass by to be weighed and considered as to their final destination-heaven or hell. The contingencies that must be taken into account for such an event are almost beyond our capacity to fully understand. The total sum of those who have lived on the earth is such that even if only 30 seconds, or upward to 1 minute, being set aside for each person-the number of years needed to consider everyone would boggle the mind. It would be such that eternity would be in operation an extensive amount of years with a great many souls still left waiting their turn to approach this "seat." As such, I counter with an additional add-on to the "still and silent moment" prior to our Lord's return. It only seems reasonable to ponder this.

I do believe that each person who is alive, or who has ever lived, will be in a state of dread or joy dependent upon their relationship with their Lord. Their understanding of their own conduct as well as the mitigation, or lack of mitigation (of their behaviors) due to either having (or not having) a personal, positive relationship with Him, will be the basis for these possible perspectives. As such, the fates of the masses will have already been sealed by their own conscious understanding of self as they consider self in the moments prior to His imminent return.

The paring off of the sheep from the goats will be a momentary matter of a small measure of time. The actual joy or anxiety personally experienced will be in play (and permanent) as he sets His foot on the mountain, is my position. As such, all will be where they are destined to be and it won't take a long term process to arrive at that placement. Our soul will know its destination, we will convict ourselves is entirely the case. So, this is the first responsibility I have to the reader-to provide these perspectives. I will, however, continue so that the facts become clearer to the reader.

The scriptures state that God is the same yesterday, today, and forever so it is easy to accept (by those who are willing to face His reality) that His pronouncements and admonitions as timeless, universal, and without end. Therefore, if He says something must be a certain way or that we must meet specific expectations, then that is how it is. This is without anyone being able to say that in the present age we don't do things that way, anymore. Further, that it is OK to be disobedient and rebellious and that God really doesn't mean what he has stated is delusional in nature. Unfortunately for many, this is what they accept as their truth. What was the way that life was expected to be lived in the past is equally appropriate to now; so how can we fail to face the truth of His words for the sum total of humanity throughout time? A part of this delusion is such that it confirms the addiction field definition of insanity wherein the same things are done over and over again with a different result being expected. Beyond this, they fail to heed history to their own, future realized, painful demise.

Case in point is the present policy regarding homosexuality and the demands of a liberal court system which mandates that they be allowed to marry in the United States. A look back at a very early time of Sodom and Gomorrah leave one with the reality that God abhors homosexual lifestyles in practice. Granted, it seems appropriate to say that we have not dipped to the same level if we give an extensive interpretation to that earlier time. Even though comparisons may be favorably drawn for now versus then, we are not able to be assured that we are substantially different in meaningful ways. The fact that it is allowed nationally and supported by the federal government and court systems, and we are forced (I do say forced-a majority of voters in many states were in opposition to the homosexual unions and marriage) to accept this as a new reality, will not be unnoticed by our Source. At what point, do we say that we have reached a plateau equal to, or within close proximity to, the limits of our Creator tolerance for sin? I do not feel that it is something that I would wish to challenge my God with but, are we not doing just that? This is something to consider in the context of the adage that those who do not learn or remember the lessons of history are doomed to repeat it.

Finally, scripture states that man will become lovers of man and this is also apparent with the vast majority of people's daily attention given to other human personalities. This is in comparison to a concurrent avoidance of equal (or even close approximate) concern and attention to a personal relationship with the Father and Son. We demonstrate a love and adoration for; athletes, musicians, movie and television actors, politicians, and artists of all types. Further, we spend our time with entertainment as well as other distractions derived from substances, pursuit of material possessions, and sensual pleasures. Meanwhile, many demonstrate a general, base ignorance of even the most elementary scriptural tenants. There are those who attempt to obey our Creator's words, yet common social expectations are for those individuals to just keep placing monies into the tax coffers and, otherwise, remain silent.

This is apparent when one considers the actions of humanity; even though now some are on the cusp of actually blatantly verbalizing the disgust which is hidden in their hearts who feel offended and constrained by compliance with God's prohibitions. Rather than read the Bible, many hurl insults at others who quote its contents. The common suggestion is that those who depend on the Bible for guidance are somehow rigid, ignorant, and ill-informed by most liberal-oriented, present-day, secularly-led individuals (often in the media). The Bible was responsible for providing stable, logical, and rational thought-based behaviors in the past that are now frequently absent as the book has been deemed archaic by present standards and draws dust on shelves. Now we just "feel."

So, how did this happen? We have perceptually altered our understanding of ourselves and our world. We "feel" rather than concern ourselves with how we "behave." We align and give allegiance to science rather than religion, worship man rather than God, and rely on our governmental agencies and politicians for our support and nurturing (instead of churches and clergy). Many place their ultimate value on things which may rot, rust, or crumble instead of having a preference for a beneficial, eternal status. A common ideal when I was a lad was that winning was important and that ideal was the primary goal of our effort and participation. Now, one only "tries," then they get a trophy. (In fact, a client told me that his brother got a trophy even though he had been disqualified and disallowed from competing while in school-go figure?) When I was a young enlisted airman, during an era of combat, we were trained that when we were instructed to "take a position" we had to actually take the position-"trying" didn't cut it. I fear that we are planting the seeds to a malaise which will lead to our defeat and ruination due to such insanity. Maybe not right away, but the writing appears to be on the wall.

We see this resignation for just getting by, or being content with less that our best efforts, on a daily basis. The fact that there is a safety net known as government programs results in there being no urgency to provide for oneself (or do our best). Those who attempt to provide for themselves are required to also carry on their backs an equal number of their fellow citizens. These people see their "rights" as absent any "obligations" for self to attempt to provide for their own needs. Scripture states that failure to do so is being "worse than an infidel"; they were out to lunch when that lesson was being taught, I surmise.

We see it daily where excuses and explanations replace results and honorable conduct. The exercise of placing "value" for many things is in an assigned dollar amount; not understanding that those things of true value cannot be purchased with money. We are forever seeking knowledge, yet, failing to arrive at the truth as scripture indicates will be our lot. Further, we have viewed barbaric behaviors and make empty promises to redeem the afflicted that will be ignored when a strong backbone requires actions by our leaders. Yet, we have really "progressed" as we run towards an end that is consistent with those other civilizations which became top-heavy. This has been described as placing a "yoke on the shoulders of the people that weights them down unnecessarily" (paraphrased words of Christ during his time on Earth). This is not dissimilar to the present time with the regulating obsessions of government-its agencies, departments, and branches at multiple levels of governance attempting to make their existence relevant (?). Christ also refused to answer his detractors when his "trial" was accomplished in the dead of night (since evil avoids the light it has been theorized). Do you wonder why? Let me try to explain.

Further evidence of the similarity of that past time to the present is seen with a similar mindset in operation by those who provide this "yoke" to those now governed. Christ did not answer his accusers due to what appears obvious to me; they were so proud, arrogant, and conceited that an answer would have been useless. Why bother to provide any information to those who "know everything" and are "always right"? They are so self-assured that acknowledgements of having made any mistakes, errors in judgment, or policy blunders will not occur. The simple, yet continually present, practice that I observe in the modern era is that practically no one will just state that they made a mistake and offer an apology.

Peter was instructed that we need to forgive 7 times 70 yet there is an important thing to add to this explanation regarding forgiveness. The one being forgiven actually must first acknowledge that they are wrong, apologize, further ask for forgiveness sincerely, and then depend on decency and goodwill of those who were offended by the misbehavior to offer forgiveness. This just doesn't happen since being wrong is not perceived as possible therefore an act of forgiveness is not only unnecessary; without the acknowledgement of error, it lets the guilty one off the hook. This results in a lack of understanding of the human, errant imperfection that they hide and ignore regarding themselves. This is why God may now be considering that we have indeed went beyond reason and allowable conduct with no remorse and attempt to correct our present state. Scripture further states we are to humble ourselves, pray for, and seek mercy but this does not seem possible for the masses who blame everyone but themselves when there is a problem.

So, to consider these things it is important to consider the simple fact that the human organism in our society has altered the functional basis of their existence. They have replaced reason, right/wrong, and truth with emotions, opinions, and feelings; facts no longer matter. Reality is that many are not able to provide available, legitimate facts to support the babbling of a world with a compulsion to speak without self-respect for their lack of knowledge. As you read Part 2, The Modern Perceptual Shift (Preference for Emotional-Responses as Reality), realize that our time is not infinitum. Unless we face the understanding that a return to sanity, absent the fanaticism of a liberal-mindset based on the idea of having "rights" and comfort without reasonable, obvious duties and obligations, we will have "a rough road to hoe."

Ignorance of the dangers inherent with disregard for God's plan will not provide us any "cover" from his responses to the many who disrespect him at practically all turns in present-day culture. It is due to our own reliance on emotions while lacking in reasoned, appropriate behavior that will result in a deserved response from God. Scripture states that life will be going on and no one will notice until it is, in actuality, too late but this is the folly that a lack of an adequate attention span will leave the irreverent with. A failure to focus on our world, and a demonstrated ignorance of our subservient place to our Creator, will not lead to having one of our best days when he pulls the proverbial "plug."

We will be left to rue our indiscretions when we are called on after that moment of "total silence and stillness." Christ frequently stated that those who have eyes-see; and those who have ears-hear. Some of the created has failed to respond to his plea to use the senses provided by our Creator; his instructions have been largely dismissed. Only when the time of the deluge will the full weight of his response to our rebellion be felt by those who live for the moment. I pray for his mercy and hope that some will be allowed to positively fulfill scripture that says that, "many will be called, but few will be chosen." There is even a further point of fear due to additional adage from scripture which described the later time as being, "cut short, or none would be spared." I did not write these words in His book, I am only a messenger and servant who takes seriously my responsibility to give others what I perceive to be truth. Only the individual can make a personal plea for their own self. I believe it is entirely accurate that I can state that He will listen to those who do call out-failure to do so is not an option.

As you go forward to Part 2, I ask for your indulgence in taking the time to review the material and keep intent on the concepts within. It may seem to be a professionally-intended source of information, yet the common man is well served by spending the time to review it. It is highly insightful and will give a clear picture of how we have arrived at our state as individuals, a nation, and a civilization. The over-riding theme is that we have altered our functional basis from primarily being based on reasoning and now understand ourselves and others through feelings. This is a fundamentally flawed perspective which could cause us such issues unless corrected that it is vital to, at least, be aware of the process by which this has unfolded. It is offered as a means of understanding our basis humanity and how we are altering ourselves towards an obsolete status, unless we all address this individually.

Part 2

The Modern Perceptual Shift

The Modern Perceptual Shift

(Preference for Emotional-Responses as Reality)

Introduction

I have come to realize that the shift in perceptual-based reasoning of the past 50+ years concerning the manner in which decisions were arrived at, is disturbing. (The era beginning in the middle 1960's and forward to today). Our present, predominate reliance on emotional-based reasoning (at the expense of the historical foundations of rational-based thought) will cause upheaval that is hard to predict the extent of damage from if left to continue unabated. Rational-oriented, critical-thinking, processes have been discarded as difficult, personally-obligating, and time-consuming. Due to a general absence of knowledge (app. 1/3 of the U.S. population has a formal academic education above the high school level), the end result is that what is available for a vast majority of the populace (emotions and feelings) represents the primary source of awareness which they rely upon. I can also attest to observations that a formal, advanced education does not ensure any preponderance of abilities to reason in all cases. Understand, there are many with vocational trainings to manage and operate various needed, skilled-worker, operations. Yet, our "education" has become a means of separation from our origins as we "know" everything (thus, irreverence ensures); this is absent a fundamental reasoned application typical with more traditional, scriptural sources.

Due to the sophisticated nature of our modern technological society this lack of advanced knowledge by the remaining 2/3rds means that they operate primarily based on an emotional nature, often absent sufficient reason. In past times, Bible reading and scriptural-based instruction was more extensive and resulted in the existence of basic foundation for reasoned, rational-thinking. This fundamental understanding of what makes up a spiritual life was imbedded in cultural, societal operation. There is not this moderating, directive influence present as participation and study of scripture is not reflected in a majority of society. It does not currently seem to be considered relevant, appreciated, and prized. In actuality, God does not seem to have the same value as in this previous time based upon actual behavior where his pronouncements regarding living standards have been voided. Some do value their source yet their numbers are of dubious preeminence. (Present reading habits indicate that over 450 million copies of a series of books from a backdrop of witchcraft are one of the most popular reads in civilized, western culture over a recent, 10-year, period).

What has occurred, due to a multi-faceted, multi-disciplined shift with all parts to the puzzle functioning primarily in this present state, may prove to be detrimental to our stability. This will adversely affect ongoing sustainability for civilized society. I will develop a general discussion of the dynamics of this lopsided extreme towards emotional considerations. However, an additional concern is to address the individual in therapy. This read will enlighten many regarding the dysfunction present in the individual's daily life. The goal is to provide a means for the person to have a more productive, less-cumbersome (and less painful) alternative to this "modern," irrational, emotional-based reasoning as reality.

Prelude to & Beginning
of the Problem

In the 1950's, prior to the suggested perceptual change for understanding of what was of value regarding reality, the prevalence was for behavioral and thought-based psychological activities. Problem-solving (critical-thinking skills), scriptural adages, and behavioral modification (shaping personality) were in vogue. They constituted the established norms for understanding our motivations, thinking, and actions. The illogical basis that we are motivated primarily by emotional-based assessment of our lives was not considered until approximately the middle of the 1960's. The idea that one must be happy and feel good was not a mandate, it was optional and secondary with the success of the society trumping individualism. The interest in self and emotional expression as the norm was deemed being selfish. (At that time being self-centered was frowned upon and punished socially). The idea of being happy was attached to the ideal of being content, satisfied, and grateful. This happiness was connected with the successful occurrence of events, milestones, etc. that signified the accomplishments and joys associated with the family and/ or with self-fulfillment of achieved objectives.

These objectives typically included the interests of others equally as it did for the advantage of the individual. Thus, the experienced happiness was a deep and meaningful self-satisfaction absent the distorted sense of "pleasure" found from that perceived with substance use. In the "modern" time that had not yet arrived, the idea of happiness and pleasure had not became based on a sensual or cognitively-distorted experience from ingestions of drugs that altered the brain chemistry pattern of the individual. The prosperity and increase in available time that ensued due to the inventions and advances of technology allowed for experimentation. The self, personal expression, and experimentation with the inventions of the era (including drugs) allowed for self-absorbed, inward-directed self-interest based on trying out perceptual amending substances and alternatives to a connection to our origins.

At the beginning of the period in question (mid-1960's and moving forward), the basis for mental health treatment broadened, shifted, and diverted towards an addition of emotions to understand ourselves. This treatment was deemed important and was based on the idea that feelings were an essential means of understanding the behaviors of humans. Within the new form of information presentation (the televised media), emotions were promoted. Those practitioners who assisted individuals who had distress based on mental health concerns (as depicted on television) focused primarily on feelings (emotions). This occurred due to the universally accepted idea that individuals had to be happy. This was the new norm and existential gold standard. The societal rule became that "one must be happy and, if not, then they must take steps to become happy." Happiness ("feeling good") was the prime consideration and the new reality or goal for living (an emotional state).

The primary statement used to stereotype the mental health professional, in their work with clients, was the clinician asking the client, "how do you feel?" or "how does that make you feel?" This is also the barb or pun directed at a friend who states to their associates that he intend to see, or is seeing, a mental health therapist. (This is in comparison to the previous time when common expression was, "what were you thinking?" This was my parent's response in their questioning of my childhood misbehaviors in the late 1950's. This preference for thinking (rather than feeling) was the represented perceptual reasoning at that time).

If one were to dispute this seemingly apparent perceptual change from having happiness optional and desired after safety, security, and deficit needs being achieved, then consider this. In conversations that occurred at that time, and has increasingly become common place since then, the invariable question asked during conversations between people is "are you happy," or, "why are you not happy," or, "why are you sad"? The apparent results of ease and comfort that our new social systems, and technological advances, allowed for included a newly determined interest in happiness (emotional state). As a tendency to go to extremes in conduct (dichotomies) is common for humanity, we discarded thinking for an essential shift to feelings to account for our valuing of the human condition. This is theorized as being associated with an advancing society achieving its fullest completion by our secular progressives. Instead, we have opened up the proverbial "hornet's nest" of issues we are still only recently being able to partially realize. The idea took hold that not feeling good about doing something made it alright to ignore or avoid the responsibility to do the "right" thing.

This presentation and forwarding of the utility of mental health treatment and how it was effective to assist the distressed person transformed a cottage industry (talk therapy) into a financially-viable means of income to providers of these services to society. Many professions owe their overall existence to this new need for services that is essentially predicated on overwhelmingly considering, weighting, and discussing of feelings. This new industry relied on the value of emotion as a basis of good mental health (feeling good and being happy) to expand its reach and growth. Should one wish to contest the idea that emotion is the basis for this industry, they only need look at the trade manual used by mental health therapist and professionals, the DSM which has multiple editions. The DSM, or, *"Diagnostic and Statistical Manual of Mental Disorders"* lists all recognized mental-related dysfunction. The actual effect of considering emotion as the basis for providing mental health treatment services becomes clear in a review of this manual. Should one exclude those DSM-identified, mental health disorders that were directly (or indirectly) related to emotion (or emotional-based behaviors) then they would have but a mere flimsy pamphlet, in both size and content.

Societies Changing
Basis of Support

It is also vitally important to note that, prior to this change in the source of support towards counseling of a psychological nature, the emphasis of support was primarily based upon being good (a behavior)-rather than feeling good (an emotion). Only recognize that the prior means of support for distress was, up until the middle 1960's more often provided by clergy (or spiritually-related staff). (Now, increasing less common as we advance into the present century). Then, doing the "right thing" took precedence over "feeling better" even though one knew that doing the right thing did not always make us feel better. The earlier reality was that we didn't have a choice based on feelings, we knew that since it was right we had to comply. One comes to an awareness that it is becoming increasing more common for at shift from spiritual answers to distress to be replaced with psychology, and secular-based counseling, so that one will feel better. (We actually find present-day segments entertaining the idea that we are not a nation of laws but must consider "gray areas" associated with emotional- reasoning, instead of reasoned-rational thoughts). Thus, the assertion of feeling good being the new interest that was based on emotional comfort.

This new reality is at the expense of the previously practiced, long-term, commitment more often connected to doing the "right" thing. That commitment fulfilled a long-term goal of connecting to a spiritual source (Father and the Son) in that earlier time. When short-term, immediate basis for functioning known as instant gratification becomes common place; morality, right reason, law and societal order, and stability are compromised for feelings, pleasure, and emotional-reasoned approach to the world. This new reality found long-term commitment for a number of aspects of life (work, marriage, and faith) to be archaic and perceived as difficult and overly-consuming due to the need to sacrifice for others ahead of self. In fairness, there are a measurable portion of the populace that remain committed to scriptural, spiritual resources for support. Reality is that the number living in this manner continue to decrease as each generation continues into the future. (Some may argue that we are remaining steady, or increasing spiritually, yet what one now considers as spiritual in nature is far removed from the reality of its origins that included obedience to our source).

This new emphasis on emotion has had multiple negative effects on society; both as a civilized basis of existence as well as in the lives of each individual who lives within this ongoing degeneration of our world. First-consider the effects on society. To begin, having to be happy and, when not happy, doing what is deemed appropriate to become happy has led to the explosion of drugs-both legal and illegal, in our society. An initial media portrayal was that one needed to "take a pill and everything would be alright" (in its most elementary beginnings in advertisement the idea was that chemistry equated with improving our lives-shortly thereafter, the results of chemistry (pharmacy products) followed as making lives better; then onward to the present). As time continued, drugs of all types became the new norm. In a previous time the young adults stated that they did not take "poison" (how they interpreted drugs to be in essence-circa. 1960), later, experimentation with substances became "cool" and socially expected as one closed in on adulthood. (This occurred towards the end period of 1960's, and continues onward). Understand that roughly close to 90% of the anti-depressant prescribed occur in the United States-although we make up a small overall percentage of the world population. This statistical representation is similar with most mental health treatment medications for the range of mental health diagnostic-group drug treatments.

The general, common thought process was that drugs make us "feel good" rather than actual fact that they may often allow for a distorted reality originating within our cranial regions. Being appropriate is secondary to feeling appropriately-or so seems to be the moniker for this new perceptual reality. As such, feeling good serves as the motivation for behaviors and drugs support realizing this goal. One lives in a distorted sense of reality with various portions of the brain over, or under, stimulated. This lack of understanding by the general populace that substances actually moderate or intensify the brain cell neurotransmitters to various degrees leads to the idea that drugs are the direct and total cause of our perceptually altered experience. Instead, the event of usage is the beginning to a process that cause the integrity of the cranial region to be compromised to a degree (and duration) that may, in many instances, have long-term detrimental effects. The absence of future drug use does not fully mitigate the damage and this reality is not understood by the abuser of substances who may be rendered a burden on society by this lack of awareness. This damage may extend to multiple generations into the future of which we are only now seeing the societal impact from the advent of the drug culture.

Additionally, entertainment is engaged in a basis distraction from reality by the attention to non-productive or non-sustaining deviations to account for their perceived "free time." This is in spite of the reality that sizeable segments of civilization suffer and have unmet basic needs that we would be well-served to address with whatever time that is available. Instead, entertainment serves as another option for "pleasure" while disregarding our duties to humankind. Finally, materialistic interest round out a general consideration of behavior being directed at "feeling good" and buying or owning stuff somehow allows for that "pleasure" to occur. The result is that all of these distractions allow one the avoidance of the reality that, possibly, they may not behave properly or feel well. Further, human suffering continues to exist and many have unresolved problems in their individual lives.

Drug use has led to a portion of the DSM being written to diagnostically identify substance abuse and dependence as it relates to multiple illicit drugs uses. Further, the extent of abuse and continued escalating use of prescription medications, is having a deteriorating effect on social order that only grows and increases as the generations traverse across the stage of our civilization's developmental trajectory (along with the illegal substance addictive habits). Essentially, because we have to "feel" good (emotion state), and its primary basis for expressing a "good life" presently, we experience many aspects of our societal dysfunction that only getting one's needs met lead us to. Also to be noted, the DSM has much content from the dysfunction that has been self-medicated with these substances to address other mental health issues. This is commonly referred to as a dual-diagnosis issue. This issue involves the drug use as well as the initial, or subsequent, additional mental health diagnostic issue that co-exists; from either before (or after) the drug habit's beginning. Not only are mental health issues potentially an occurrence; physical illnesses and dysfunction are such that disability may be long-term, or total.

Mental Health Therapy: A Functional Basis of Understanding

This evolving theory of emotion as a basis for understanding (thus the resulting behavior) is taught in classrooms to the therapist in training who will becomes the treatment specialist in the field of mental health services. This training is based on the presently, most popular modality that is also used for framing research into the study of the mind, is known as CBT (cognitive-behavioral therapy). Essentially, the advent of the cognitive-behavioral therapy approach (which has mushroomed to a place of supremacy as the primary evidence-based, preferred treatment of choice for mental health issues) began the slant toward what became an overvaluing of emotion (although indirectly at first).

As academic literature requires citation of other's materials it would be only appropriate to acknowledge that two biblical scriptural excerpts are at the core of CBT's inception I believe. This is rather than the common, secular identity of the 1970's suggested basis for invention by, among others-Aaron Beck. First, scripture states that "there is nothing new under the sun" (Ecclesiastes 1:9, NKJV) and, generally, all things occur "over and over again." (As such, also note that my expressions and information provided within this treaties may have been expressed by many other individuals who have seen that which I am writing about. They may understand equally as well these observations, or may be even better able to explain them). The second scriptural adage is that, "as he thinks, in his heart, so he is" (Proverbs 23:7, NKJV). This clearly and rather succinctly states the conceptual basis for CBT. The actual "equation" (common conceptual equation of the process of the mind's operation) is that;

(a) An individual thinks a thought, then, (b) has a feeling (emotion) based on the individual's perceptional consideration of that, or other resultant, thought and thus, (c) leading to frequently acted upon behavior that is based on an interest in satisfaction of the emotional feelings that they have, and may often continue to experience.

(1st Step) Thoughts➜ (2nd Step) Emotions➜ (3rd Step) Actions

The literature on the CBT method as presented by its theoretical founder and his family member, Judith Beck, (in the textbook entitled-*"Cognitive Therapy: Basics and Beyond"),* was that essentially thoughts (Step 1) occurred on at least 3 levels. The individual may blurt out an expression as a response to something or someone. Then, we must realize that there was some idea (rule) behind that blurting out that serves as the literal basis for the errant expression. Finally, (at its deepest level) typically a source from developmental origins, a foundational belief system ideal, or a shared value, or virtue learned as a child is the start point for the ideas associated with our thoughts. Further, consider that there were various irrational (or dysfunctional) thought-based categories where the blurted out, belief/rule, or foundational ideals are illogical, ineffective, or inappropriate ways of thinking or understanding our world. These various listing of the actual categories as they relate to improper or ill-conceived thinking types usually are listed with between 13, and upward to 16, different dysfunctional thought-based categories (on average by my personal experience of study). There may be more, or less, in number of categories depending on what source you read, but the point is that there appears to be a finite number of thought-related categories to consider.

(1st Step) Thoughts, ➜ (3 levels-surface to deepest). (a.) blurted statement – to, (b.) rules that support the blurted out statement – to, (c.)

beliefs that are the foundational, developmental basis for the individual's existence and rules.

One should consider the talk therapy session as it unfolds. This equation unfolds and forms the therapeutic basis, loosely, to uncover and consider the parts to the thinking, feeling, behavioral-acting process that may be the source of the individual's dysfunction or diagnostically identified mental issues. It is theorized that an assessment of the human functional process, as just identified, will lead to successful (and optimal) correction to dysfunction. The initial thoughts, and as they relate to forming the emotions, requires considering whether the thoughts were accurate, important, relevant, etc. This determines the appropriateness, or need, for the emotion(s) that the client is feeling. Beyond the initial concern for the thought; a more intense concern for the resultant emotion frequently serves as the follow-up and continuation of therapy as described by much CBT training materials.

(Step 1) Thoughts, ➔ (is it true?) Is the blurted thought, underlying rule, and foundational belief appropriate, relevant, or reasonable? If not, reconsider thought without even going to the further steps of emotion (Step 2), or, behavior/action (Step 3).

The central concern for this scenario is that one must apply what one is thinking and, then secondly, follow up by considering the emotions of the person. This is then, lastly, results with the actions of the person as a result of emotional-based response to the initial thoughts. The fact that emotional-based reasoning is utilized to come to a course of action is very troubling for a number of very real, serious reasons. (I have found that, in providing therapy to clients, they uniformly and consistently acknowledge that their emotional outbursts, that they describe as being "absent thinking" has detrimental effects on their lives. Further, they acknowledge that the emotions are ineffective in addressing their problem successfully). The suggestion for the equation is that it is a primarily linear formulation that begins with a thought, to feelings (emotion), and concluding with action (behavior) is at the root of the problem.

Doing so includes the idea that the solution is arrived at by making the emotion-based response a higher level stage that was the follow-up to the initial thought (Step 2 of the equation as primary over the Step 1). The result is that, reasoning and critical-thinking (Step 1) are suggested to be disregarded as the sole, total, or primary source leading to the action/behavior (Step 3), and that emotion (Step 2) must be a major player in the solution and considered predominate to any conclusions by many.

Even though we can readily acknowledge that we often use reason (Step 1) to form actions (Step 3); the act of feelings (Step 2) leading to our behaviors cannot be defended due to an inadequacy that is obvious to this writer. Granted, thinking is considered as it related to the appropriateness or accuracy of the thoughts that have occurred as the first step to the equation. However, the follow-up step of emotions do not receive the same level of address (many manuals or clinical training programs suggest that they "just are" and "don't have to make sense"). Their counterbalance to thinking is represented as an uneven equilibrium with emotions caring more weight, I suppose. Their routine considered preference, rather than having emotions serving as a novel slant on the total picture, is illogical and overrated. Emotional-based behavior such as depressed mood, undeserved or nonessential anxious concern, over-excited presentation, angry outbursts, etc. represent a way the emotion plays out in its' behavioral components. I ask a client that, if you do not have an apple tree (emotion)-Can you have an apple (feeling-related dysfunction). Obviously, not. So, failure to value, consider, or depend on emotional-reasoned behaviors seems logical (at though-based perspective), or so it follows.

So that there cannot be an argument at this point, only ask-is beginning a cigarette smoking habit to counter stress and anxiety (emotionally-based response) that, over time, leads to cancer that ends life, a sound decision? Or, is using drugs to deal with pain (or to be accepted by peers) wise when often abuse and addiction may result? The examples can be added to yet it seems self-evident that emotion as a means of making decisions that lead to poorly-conceived behavior is not inherently useful. Point being, when thought (Step 1) and rational thinking is not fully employed, or the primary source of decision-making, the outcomes are not usually most effective. Our witness of the offspring without a parent present (out of wedlock or due to divorce) that often times results from sensual, emotionally-directed seeking of pleasure absent a mature, responsible relationship represents a serious, painful consequence. The parents which did not operate with a sufficient rational, reasoned basis that would have been based on getting to know each other and making reasonable efforts to be certain of their permanency to their relationship prior to engaging in an intimate way that led to the child being born. If shared beliefs, values, and thoughts had occurred sufficiently this would be less likely to occur. Or, due to a common lack of sufficient thinking of ways to compromise, couples routinely separate; thus, leaving the child in the lurch. It represents another constant reminder of the outcome of emotionally-based behaviors often without mature, rational decisions based on thinking rather than feeling.

So as to disallow counter-arguments, it is also appropriate to realize that how one "feels" about going to work or providing for their needs will have no effect on their having their needs satisfied. If one does not "feel" like going to work (and acts on that feeling) it will not turn out well when the financial obligations are unmet. The results are not positive with a host of possible negative consequences available that can be devastating. (Being hungry, ill-health, homelessness, repossession, fines, crime, etc.). This argument can be applied to a myriad of circumstances such as going to a doctor when ill, what we eat as healthy, taking care of obligations at work, school, or in a relationship, etc. Yet, "feeling" is not central to success in more instances than not- results take priority over emotional-based responses. "Feeling good" is not the end consideration, or most prevalent aspect, to these issues.

The use of consideration of feelings from the initial emotions (from which the feelings find their origins) represents the basis for therapy for many therapists that I have consulted with. Emotions "just are" and anyone can consider them, or so the newly-trained, aspiring therapist concludes based on many training experiences. Further, my observation is that the novice, less-seasoned, or therapist of limited work-related hours rely on "how do you feel" in absence of therapy practice that examines thoughts and rational-based thinking processes. Emotional/

feeling related reflections represent a reliable stand-by for questioning or discussion when the therapy work tends to arrive at a stuck point or when there is an embarrassing, long silence. When one considers the ever-expanding growth to the field of mental health services you can clearly see how the trend continues to expand towards emotion (increasing demand for services and limited number of seasoned practitioners) and away from the predominance of thinking to reach sound, rational-based conclusions.

This is when the extent of life experience of the new therapist who does not have sufficient life-skills tools to fully cultivate thought-based functional basis that investigate the deeply-held, early-lifetime foundational, rules that the client makes decisions from. Clients have fine-tuned their rules over a lifetime and only critical assessments of their thinking processes can serve to positively consider the issues requiring therapy. This is absent an overloaded discussion of emotional-reasoned actions which have become the genesis to therapy. The lack of sufficient training in problem-solving strategies and of critical-thinking skills, along with the lack of a sufficient quality and quantity of life experiences, limits the effectiveness of the therapeutic process. The result is that the therapy session, fundamentally, becomes an exercise in the sharing of emotions to account for the majority of the therapeutic work. As each succeeding generation of therapist take their place in the field, the reliance on emotional reasoning and considering feelings becomes more entrenched in the therapy work as being of significance.

The problem for this explosion of feelings, emotion, and pleasure can be found by the initial promotion by media, and expanded upon to provide a revenue for those who learn the skills to work in the field, with an approach for emotions. Since the media and public holds such a value on emotions to understand people, the follow-up is that emotions are believed to be a reasonable way of considering our world and it provides a means for everyone to participate (absent any critical-thinking skills or actual education, training, or knowledge of actual facts). The advent of emotion to determine our world is seen in a triad of ways that, individually and collectively, have invaded most all aspects of civilization in very detrimental ways. (There is a like-wise triad associated with rational, critical-based thought as well that is counter to it and an opposite in utility and result). The view of thinking and emotion as separate entities in the process of humans to make decisions forms a basis dichotomy to our existence.

Dichotomy of Objective vs. Subjective Basis for Reality

Previously to the modern era, one just didn't give feelings much impact on the decisions as survival was not assured and facts did not allow for distractions based on how one felt about those facts. A common statement from an earlier time was, "just the facts." Our new-founded comfort has allowed for us to consider our feelings and avoid facts that do not support our preferences, or so it seems to be our new social reality. Since the suggested impression is that "life is good" and "the heat is off" we can just "have fun"; we have our present situation. The terminally destructive result of failure to consider our survival and security will not allow for a "do over." I believe that this game ender is an appropriate potential deduction of our future fate, left unchecked.

If one based their actions on thoughts they must be fundamentally driven by the consideration of objective reality. Objective reality finds its origins in facts, figures, information of an exact and precise nature. There is no room for how one feels about it; 2 plus 2 always equals 4, and how one feels about 4 doesn't change the reality of it being 4. Facts and figures lead to determinations as to whether something is "right" or "wrong," not if it fits how we want or feel about a circumstance, fact, or problem. Further, right or wrong have historically been seen as the means to arrive at "truth." Truth does not allow for behavioral techniques to be developed to arrive at; it is a generally clear and from a direct application of the facts. (See- behavioral techniques later in treaties). The central "fact" about truth is that it is neutral and does not allow anyone a preference or privilege. Everyone involved is equally affected and no one has a leg up on others (unless truth is their means of approaching the circumstance, fact, or problem and others do not base their positions on those same truths or fact-based reasoning). If you operated based on truth in a previous time you were assured of being in a good space- unlike present possibilities. Before, not liking truth did not mitigate its impact on your life yet feelings are now the new, consistent, basis for actions.

(1st Step) Thoughts = (triad of facts, right-wrong dichotomy, truth w/ objective reality (logic) as basis of understanding environment).

On the opposite hand, emotion has its origins in subjective reality. Since there is no predominance based on facts, figures, or information that has to be proven to be true, one can behave because they "feel" a certain way. They don't have to rationally justify their behaviors-thus, no accountability. How one "feels" about 4 is more important than whether 2 plus 2 equals 4 (as the belief that 2 plus 3 equals 4 is likewise, just as reliable for feelings); facts are not the basis of decision as reasoning based on thoughts from critical-thinking have been discarded in preference for "how I feel." Right and wrong aren't the basis of the decision, rather, the decision comes based on how it promotes what one wants or what one prefers in the situation. Avoiding unpleasant feelings or emotions, or prolonging those feelings or emotions that one enjoys, becomes the motivation for behavior.

Try engaging in a discussion with someone when you are armed with the facts and they tell you they "feel" differently-nothing gets done and our knowledge falls on deaf ears in modern times. Any attempts at discussion are antagonized by a lack of logic with feelings being the responses to reasoned concerns. Commonly you will see the individual who relies on these feelings resorting to emotionally-based, derogatory labels directed at the person who has employed reason out of a realization that their feelings carry no weight. If they can confuse the issue then they can "control" others (self-evident in present political verbiage). They demonstrate a reliance on an illogical preferences (without facts) due to the unsupported subjective opinion they express. This demonstrates a lacking in common sense and routinely uses few accurate available tools for defense of "feelings." (See- behavioral techniques-following in text).

(1st Step) Thoughts ➔ (2nd Step) Emotions = (triad of feelings, pleasure, emotional response as basis from subjective reality (opinions) as a basis of understanding environment).

The Paradigm: Allowing Our Emotional-Reasoned Basis

The missing link to my consideration to this treaties was, for a long time that of understanding, the preeminence of emotion in humans. Why is emotion so prevalent in our social world and why do most rely on it rather than the literal basis for our superiority over the animal world? (The ability to employ reason). The most general and accurate response is, most people do not have much else to use to make decisions often times when they are not trained or skilled to use (or possess) an expertise to be able to rely on that would lead to reason or rational thinking. When you lack sufficient education or knowledge to participate in a conversation (or discussion) where reason and facts are used to consider what is in our best interests, all you have is emotional outbursts or trying to pull someone's heartstrings to try to gain an advantage and win the debate. Idle speculation of emotional-based consideration of our world is the frequent norm. Since people often times fail to acknowledge their lack of understanding on things and have a need to be involved in life (absent knowledge), they give what they have; unsupported ideas, emotionally-based reasoning, and the associated personal feelings. Since being silent makes people uncomfortable (even though my childhood lesson was to remain silent to allow for a doubt as to my lack of knowledge on a topic), they frequently maintain a compulsion to talk and express them self. End result being that emotions are the basis form of interactions in our social world.

***Please note, it appears that reasonably one could surmise that both the (Step 1) thoughts, along with the (Step 2) emotions, would allow for a balanced means of deriving a solution (Step 3 behaviors/ actions) and, as such, represents the best of both worlds. We would use rational thinking and apply the "valuing exercise" (an appropriate use of emotional considerations), from "like/approval/acceptance" across the spectrum towards the opposite end and "dislike/disapproval/refuse." This gives us the initial acceptance or rejection as a preference (emotional weighting) to be a part of fully considering the instance in question. However, in spite of this emotional weighting, we need to keep a cool head (absent errant-misguided repose) and rely on reasoning separate of the use of an excess valuing from the emotional context. Instead, my point is that present reality relies on a linear equation with the emotional portion as the follow-up and higher-leveled reasoned continuation, rather than in secondary partnership to rationally-reasoned thoughts. As such, along with present cultural reality-emotion is given an undeserved and overvalued place above thought and reason. Emotion is the supreme step for decision-making as "feeling good" is superior to doing what may be "right" from thinking. This is the actual, essential concern and reason for this treaties as well as the basis for my dark fear for our evolving detrimental reasoning strategy. (The universal rule that they must "feel good" requires involvement in discussion, decisions, or policy to protect this interest and predisposition for the objective of pleasure. Their participation is conversations is frequently guided with this rule in mind).

The Perceptual Shift:

The Impact on Society

Little additional discussion is needed to come to the conclusion that feelings, pleasure, and emotion have become the new norm. It allows whoever that has the majority support of others (by using emotional-based reasons or arguments to the public to gain support-mob mentality) to be able to secure their goals, objectives, and policy interests. This utilized emotional context ensures control of society. The problem that is resultant from this approach is that the ideals of efficiency, effectiveness, competence, superiority, etc. are connected to forwarding the interests of ensuring a pleasurable, positive feeling (or enjoyable emotional experience for the individual) rather than of rational-based, mutual benefit for everyone. The need to solve issues and ensure the security and interest of all have become secondary to this rule of feeling good and experiencing pleasurable emotional life for self and like-minded, emotionally-led people. In present operation, preeminence in society is based on the slogan "long live the coalition." This leads to a discussion of how the advent of dependence on emotion has effects on our social structure that has the potential to be critically destructive (unless seriously considered and effectively addressed).

Control in government, law, criminal justice, media, business, education, and most all additional areas of society have become affected by "feelings" and emotional-based reasoning. It seems appropriate to state that only those things such as accounting, mathematics, statistics, and engineering (where there is a lack of emotion that defers to the use of numbers instead), is reason still in force. When one wants to run the government they need to have the majority of the electorate to run government in a democracy, or do they? Fundamentally, the general mechanisms of representative government are presently run by the appeal to emotion that pits various hyphenated groups of identified citizens, as opponents. The actual goal is to form a coalition that allows one to have control and this is how things have increasing become in representative democracy. Instead of right of center (or left of center), the actual representations that make the political options are at each extreme of a continuum. With emotional reasoning, labels, and generalizations are employed to strategize for an advantage at gaining emotional-based support to gain, or maintain, control.

American political theory for representative government was significantly based on John Locke's writing that stated that (among other things) we had "inalienable rights from God." However, the "from God" portion of the phrase has been omitted as of approximately 1963 in actual, social practice. Our moderating factors associated with public display of the Ten Commandments, school and public prayer, and deference for scriptural prose was initially diminished and, now, fundamentally absent from social operation. Now, there is no "level playing field" where all are measured by the same, like expectations from scriptural directives. As such, who is in charge deems what constitutes our "rights" and those in power frequently find favor for "rights" for those who support them over those who do not. Specifically, it is not routine to see those who are in the political arena fail to employ arguments that are of a rational, fact-based nature yet rely on emotionally-charged, negative characterizations of their opponents. This allows for the attempt to maintain their power or succeed with their beliefs and policies? I cannot remember when I recently heard the salutation of "my fellow American" as leaders appear to no longer consider all-only their supporters routinely receive acknowledgements.

Further, when representation is not the issue, and those in power can assign the individuals who support their ideals to positions of appointments in the courts, administrative agencies, etc., the use of emotion is employed. Emotional arguments forward the agenda within those appointed areas to defend, support, or explain legislation, legal decisions, or legal codifications that are representative of a particular political groupthink that they owe their position to. Common, emotionally-related themes to promote their agendas ("spin") are to protect the weak from the "tyranny of the masses" or to allow for marginal groups to have "individual freedoms" that are not supported by cultural tradition of the people that form the basis for the authority of our elected officials to govern. This allows to provide what they presume as appropriate explanations for playing groups off on other segments of society. They may not represent the majority group in their own right, but in the cumulative coalition numbers banded together, result in achieving control over the traditional interests and principles of the government. This ensure the positive, personal expression of pleasure associated with being in control over others and "having one's way." This also ensures that they get their needs met as the top priority; frequently in opposition to our traditions and long-standing moral standards. Further, when emotion rules over reason then the result leads to a total insanity where things fail to be right or wrong, make sense based on reason or facts, or ensure a lack of anarchy or promote a continuing survival.

In criminal justice the idea of "swift and sure punishment" and that the "punishment fits the crime" have been negatively affected by emotions also. Consider that the process of justice is agonizing in its' slow pace and, further, the sentences do little to reflect the actual injury. If your family member is killed your emotional response would be serious and justice would be expected for the offender. Yet, our system gives little interest in the offended party's losses and long-term suffering often times (or so it seems). Instead, taxes are spent into the millions of dollars to be used to allow for a "defense fund" for the mass-murderer. The emotional experience demonstrated by the system that has difficulty with giving strict sentencing is based on the displeasure associated with being "hard" on criminals. The negative, personally-experienced emotion for having to "judge" the criminal allows for "good time served" and "cost to society" to outweigh "truth" and "justice" as previously established during a different perceptual reality. Official statistics suggest that our crime rates are dwindling, yet, I counter that we are just avoiding our responsibilities to charge, try, and convict those committing crimes as we previously did.

We fail to uphold standards and/or maintain appropriate expectations of conduct (illegal entry into the country is ignored and culture is now considered in multiplicity rather than as a collective unit with all required to be obedient to our Creator). Whatever behavioral techniques that is available to be employed to avoid negative emotional-based feelings by those tasked with protecting the public occurs. This represents our society in operation and serves as a model for the general public to emulate. These are all emotionally considered concepts and the result is that the current state of emotional-based reasoning does not consider the base need for self-preservation of the republic. This also plays out in the actions of leaders for foreign policy as they fail to adequately consider the necessary means to secure our interests. This is because they have a concern for others' feelings, or so it seems; and where being "liked" is more vital (popularity) than being responsible.

(1st Step) Thoughts ➔ (2nd Step) Emotion ➔ (3rd Step) Actions= Gain: desired feelings ←Spin (Backward)

Common courtroom practices, where the rights and obligations of the individual are considered and the individual's ability to be judged for damages caused by self, or caused by others to self, is also an emotional-based experience. The goal of finding errors in procedural guidelines, missteps or honest mistakes being a basis for punishment, a means of defense absent the actual "truth" of being innocent or guilty, and using any means to deter or pervert attempts at expedience to respect cultural sensibilities regarding "right" or "wrong" are the examples of emotional reasoning in legal practice. Frequently, emotional displays and plays on emotions of jurors (or the public) are employed to achieve the only self-perceived importance of legal contortions, which is to "prevail." Even though we originally tried to show mercy to the guilty, rather than giving the full extent of sentencing, it has become common to see emotion used to "win" rather than serve justice to honorably consider the afflicted, and, affliction to the evil doer.

You may be totally innocent (or deserving of remedy) but "right" is not enough in the present context. Emotional representations by the opposing counsel that paints you in an unfavorable light due to the undeserved need to prevail (attempt to smear someone's name or character-after all none are "without spot or wrinkle"). This follows the idea of a primary interest in representing their client, rather than representing the "truth" of the circumstance that requires the trial. This represents the human-based (emotionally charged) new reality that is counter to traditional, rational-based, reason. Again, emotion is the tool to achieve the end whereby-the end now justifies the means. As I like to say; logic and reason has left the building. Scripture states that we are able to "be angry and do not sin" (Ephesians 4:26, NKJV), yet emotion has went to a place where reality should not conceivably go. My admonition to others is that- "at some point behaviors will actually matter" (when being weighed).

So as to completely consider the full effects of emotion, it is important to recognize the demonstrated behaviors that occur based on the emotionally-driven behavioral techniques. Although these provided basic explanations, or simple-stated terms, may have positive utility-they are not typically positive behavioral techniques. These behavioral techniques do not endear themselves to others who operate primarily from a traditional, ethical, and moral-based position which incorporated what was typically referred to as "right reason." Thus, when compared to an earlier perceptual reality when the means of making decisions was of a rational, thought-based decision-making strategy; we now have "spin." The listed behavioral techniques have the primary purpose of giving a means to secure emotional interests. The common discussions that take place in therapy indicate that the client typically uses these behavioral techniques to perpetuate or end emotional experiences depending on how they "feel." These techniques are at the heart of the conceptual basis of spin (to gain what you desire to feel or end an undesired feeling). This plays out as having (step 3) the behaviors, being accomplished to support (step 2) the emotion, essentially "in reverse" for the equation such as;

(Step 1) Thoughts ➜ (Step 2) Emotions ➜ (Step 3) Behavior/
Actions=Gain: emotional goal ⬅ Behavioral Techniques (Spin).

Behavioral Techniques:

(a.) Marginalizing, (b.) minimizing, (c.) avoiding, (d.) ignoring, (e.)
denial, (f.) perverting, (g.) contorting, (h.) confusing, (I.) manipulating,
(j.) over-valuation,(k.) under-valuation, (l.) justifications, (m.) excusing,
(n.) blaming, (o.) arguing, (p,) ruminating, (q.) dismissal, (r.) insulting,
(s.) criticize, (t.) lie, (u.) distort, or, (v.) other, like techniques to achieve
the goal of achieving preferred emotions and feelings-or the dismissing
of undesirable emotions and feelings.

** Please note: Theoretically, these techniques began as a "thought"
(Step 1) which led to accomplishing them ("Action") yet, they have an
existence when they are actions = (as behavioral techniques-Step 3).

Further, when anger, violent intentions, or destructive actions from
(Step 2) Emotions, occur as Actions (Step 3); they cannot be accepted
and will destroy much of what they interact with. There seems to be no
way of supporting the forward, linear progression of the equation from
(Step 2) Emotions, to ➜ (Step 3) Actions (violence and crime), in this
instance. These are additional techniques to achieve what emotional
state one desires yet are illogical in their mere essence.

Also, this perceptual reality includes that societal ideal that the
end justifies the means. Thus, the utility of spin in the present social
and cultural spectrum has been acknowledged and is practiced to leave
present social order formed from forwarding emotionally-charged,
public debate. The idea that the end justifies the means is laid with
the use of these behavioral techniques as useful to lead to personally
preferred emotions and feelings, thus; we behave so as to ensure that
these preferences are realized. This is a serious concern and has been
a common pattern just prior to the start of previous times in civilized
history when severe social upheaval has occurred. Only when the
stark reality of the fallacy and simple-minded behavioral patterns are

laid bare (due to the personally realized suffering) do people revert to understanding this perceptive reasoning style is a nightmare and further realize that, absent facts and reasoning, we fail to behave in a manner indicative of our birthright as being above the world's other species (from reason and executive functioning of the frontal lobe area).

The central problem is that, now, we have the ability to destroy ourselves in totality so we don't have the luxury for getting it right without due diligence; urgency is apparent in the present circumstances. And even more troubling, those who are in the positions to provide the immediately required responses seem either oblivious to the danger or unable to secure the best interest of those they serve. I cannot ignore that other elements of civilization have a like, or sometimes equal, cognitive capacity that will allow them to devise a means of destroying us; absent timely responses to their barbarism. As long as everyone "feels" OK, there is no urgency or so it plays out in everyday societal behavior.

Providing Support to the Individual

Since the societal impact has been briefly considered, a turn to the means of providing appropriate treatment to the individual client in need of mental health services is now considered. Pragmatically, what follows is an address to the perceptual shift frequently in practice how it affects the individual negatively. I have employed a method of "restating" the CBT method that allows for a "reverse move" to the equation from emotion back to reason (Step 2 backwards to Step 1). This is rather than proceeding, unimpeded, from emotion (Step 2) forward to the end result of an emotional-based, behavior/action (Step 3). As a point of note, the idea of "reverse move" is already in use from the (Step 3) backwards (spin) from Actions/Behaviors– to Emotions (Step 3 to Step 2) which either support or extinguish emotionally-related "feeling good/ bad emotional experience" objectives. (This is the actual operation of "spin" and the common pattern now in use for human efforts).

I counter that the "reverse move" should not get to the behaviors portion of the equation known as Step 3 (last stage) which may result in emotionally-based Actions, (ill-advised from poor planning) rather than rational, thought-based Actions. By going from emotion, back to thinking, (Step 2 – reverse back - to Step 1), rather than forward, (Step 2 – forward to - Step 3), we use a "reverse move strategy" which will ultimately be more effective and appropriate for our personal, (and societies), best interests. The initial acknowledgement to this strategy is that the use of emotion is trumped by reverting to rational reason (thinking-Step 1 of the equation); rather than allowing an emotional-charged behavior (Step 2 of the equation) occurring which leads to future problems when the Stage 3 (behavior/action based on emotions) is realized.

Suggested means of approach to the CBT Linear Equation: (**a "reverse" move**) is:

(Step 1) Thoughts ➔ /// **Halt Here**/// instead of going beyond (Step 2) Emotions; ➔ to ➔ (Step 3) emotionally-based, reasoned Behaviors/Actions- (Rather than from thought-based, reasoned Behaviors/Actions).

Consider- "Why" emotion is present ⬅ (rather than), "What" emotion is felt.

Secondly, I ask why they think that they have to take their thoughts onward to an emotionally-based level ("taking it somewhere") when the thought did not support an obvious reason for the emotional feeling that they experienced (rationally-justified as "true" basis for feelings). The behavioral action (Step 3) - at the conclusion of the feelings/emotions (Step 2) are, therefore, not justified. Further, the behaviors may typically end up reflecting negatively on the individual and may, in fact, be a source of ongoing embarrassment or personal pain. This is because their emotions don't accurately reflect the true degree of severity of the problem and often are in an excess to the extent of the problem. Further, emotional reasoning may come from another circumstance that is not even related to the thing under consideration. In short, they are angry or sad about something totally unrelated that could have happened a great deal of time earlier than the present situation.

If one does feel the need to experience an emotional state for the issue, make it a learning experience. The consideration should be to think "why" you feel the feeling or experiencing the emotion. It appears to be more appropriate than "what" you are feeling-no higher level reflection is typically needed to understand what one is feeling usually. (You can actually use the emotion to be the source of a growth experience to understand your formation and development of rules, ideas, and personal ideals and whether they are useful, appropriate, or accurate- or, not). As a lad my developmental track was based on an experience of not being allowed to go to an emotional level and, rather, sit at the kitchen table with my father to process what was at issue; getting emotional would not be well received; thought-reasoned results mattered. It has been my ongoing experience that this style of functioning is fundamentally sound and superior to allowing feelings to get in the way of realizing my best interests being served. Certainly this behavior is able to allow for a more positive social standing by giving it primacy in use rather than emotional outbursts. The actual basis for this can be explained in much the same way as an individual who is facing an emergency does not worry about how one feels, rather, getting through the issue successfully to preserve their best interests that may include survival (life and death events).

Finally, if you must use emotion, use the "ice cream sundae approach" to emotions, rather than "taking it there" constantly on a non-ending, daily basis. Consider that you may be taking it there every minute, of every hour, of every day, of every year, and on it goes-you get the picture. No wonder you end up needing to reboot with mental health services to deal with a state of, essentially, becoming uptight with dysfunction.(In my early days as a child, my mother referred to this behavior as "ruminating" and I was instructed to avoid this practice).

Question-if you have an ice cream sundae everyday-is it special? Conversely, if you have an ice cream sundae once a week or month-is it not then special? That is the general suggestion that I am asking my clients to consider when determining when to "take it somewhere" (forming actions and decisions from emotional expressions). It should be a special occasion rather than the functional basis of choice. To be clearer, let me continue.

The initial speck to the origins of humanity appear to have originated with a thought. The thought was either by the individual consider by them self (no one else involved), or, the thought was shared with other(s). In either instance, asking whether the emotion that is felt by considering the thought is true, is a start point to the process. (Usually feelings don't have a basis in true fact, I have found). When the thought is shared with others-the basic principles of communication are frequently in operation. This basic communication model is one of a sender, the message, and receiver. This model is employed for the purpose of the sharing of the thought. The problem is that, although the sum total possibilities that the receiver who hears the message may employ (agree, disagree, don't understand, want more information, or just don't care) may often not be what actually occurs. Often, the one hearing the message may be thinking (instead of listening) about what their response is, or, just ignores the situation entirely. This is rather than listening to the message or conversation. How can they have a deeply meaningful exchange when there is a lack of fullest attention between those involved in the communication process?

"Taking It Somewhere"

Further, I suggest to my clients that they use an additional option that people routinely activate. They, in essence, "take it somewhere" (frequently emotionally). In short, the message is not the message as far as the receiver of the message is concerned. They have altered, amended, or gone somewhere entirely unrelated to what is being said to the receiver-by the sender. This represents a major deterrence to effective communications. Not only is nothing being accomplished, when nations or alliances are involved, they may result in disagreements that have the potential to place the planet's collective security and safety at risk. A general failure to communicate serves as a primary barrier to living in our world in peace and addressing the ideals that would benefit the general populace. In operation, how one feels has been given more weight that the substance of communication. What results is ineffective interpersonal interactions that fail to address those thoughts productively.

An example that many may relate to of "taking it somewhere" involves a young woman in conversation with a potential male suitor. While the male suitor is talking to object of his interest, she is "taking it somewhere" else in her mind, such as- "does he think I am pretty, does he like me, is he smart, will he make a good father, will he love me, can I trust him, will he be a good provider, will he respect me, am I stupid, ugly, or fat, etc.." Meanwhile, he is also "taking it somewhere" as he is trying to figure out what he can say that will "win the day" and gain the object of his affections. (Or, both parties "feeling" depressed or anxious during, or after, their exchange as a result of "taking it somewhere" in their minds). Neither party is in direct, unaltered connection to what is being expressed by the other. This is how our society has "evolved" and our emotions serve as the basis for our interpretations of our interactions, often-times personalizing the interaction rather than processing the communications.

The actual, fundamental (and essential) need to be engaged in the conversation was avoided by going somewhere else with the situation. Further, it is frequently the case that the "taking it somewhere" leads to an emotional result. Further, it leads to considering that emotional context negatively for the person thinking of themselves or others in the communicating process. The final straw occurs when the one who has "taken it somewhere" gives the emotion-based judgments a legitimacy for themselves, or about others. They, in essence, see their emotional considerations of being stupid, ugly, dumb, etc. as the true reality to their lives.

(Step 1) Thought ➜ (Step 2) Emotion ➜ /// **Legitimized the emotion as "Fact"** /// and avoid the = (Step 3) thought-based, rational Action.

The fatal error becomes-finalizing of their self-judgment beliefs (or their judgments of others with emotional-reasoning as "fact") rather than thinking and acting without this emotional-based beliefs which form negative conclusions = (ongoing development of beliefs and behaviors that support **the development of mental health dysfunction such as anxiety or depression, etc.).**

When this process becomes the consistent choice and common result of the person's everyday world-mental illness and dysfunction is to be expected. Although each of us has a different tolerance level and strength of character integrity, "going to the well" too often will find us impeded and potentially demonstrating dysfunctional mental health as a result of constantly "taking it somewhere." This amount of distress that is able to be handled is commonly referred to as the "stress-tolerance level" of the individual. An additional admission that is necessary to add to the equation is that when the individuals do not practice positive self-care practices (good diet, adequate sleep, exercise, meditation, spiritual growth-related activities, and a stable, structured daily schedule) these problems have a greater chance of causing dysfunction. This results in having a weak, or poor, emotional self-regulation status that leaves them unable to effectively deal with their continual, routine "taking it somewhere" pattern.

All of these aspects resultant from emotion and lack of personal self-care are either jointly, or individually, a major cause of mental-illness and physical disorders. They frequently represent the source of what is included in the DSM as metal-illness related treatment concerns. Meanwhile, this behavior serves as the basis for other problems that are associated with, still other, disorders. The DSM identifies many disorders that are related to behaving in ways of a dysfunctional nature as a result of the legitimizing tendency that are actually indirectly related to the initial dysfunctional pattern. They end up resulting in multiple diagnostic issues with a range of medication and therapy needs. Further erosion of good health occurs when side effects from medications become a concern.

Where We Are At Present

As such, my interpretation of all of that which has been considered is that, a perceptual shift has occurred wherein feelings (emotions) are our new reality. We have (when the results are unpleasant by acting rationally) avoided or dismissed rational-based, reasoned responses to our world. Emotion is our basis for decisions (it allows one to feel good absent mutual concern for the total sum of our world). This appears to be evidenced by a decrease in virtuous-related behaviors (honesty, patience, humility, modesty, honor, etc.) by a sizeable portion of the populace that "loves" self (emotion). Before, we were admonished to love one another, now, only love of self seems to be the predominate expectation. The idea of being human (humanistic) has led to seeing self as the center of existence; absent the communal nature of the collective world civilization. Getting one's needs met is the supreme objective.

The idea of "right" and "wrong" and the necessity for "truth" to ensure the collective nature of our world is now unnecessary in this new perceptual reality; feeling good is all that matters frequently. This occurs due to the emotional basis of viewing our world that is primarily consisting of self, often absent others. As long as we can feel good then things are allowed to continue without due concern for long-term considerations. Our short-term happiness trumps the future of our existence with feeling good sufficient to relieve any fears about survival. This is the proverbial "rub."

We have a personal obligation to practice sound reasoning, thought-progression in our individual daily activities (and as a society also). Further, promoting these practices for our families and friends is essential. Communities will function more effectively, as will local and regional, national, and world civilization as a whole. My parent's questions to me of "what were you thinking" is truly at the heart of betterment of self. This is preferred to, as my grandmother would say, "flying off the handle" (emotional outburst). A common, yet appropriate, practice to reboot our cultural means of reasoning is to have expectations for ourselves and others with whom we interact. Tolerance for emotion and the illogical and damaging results of this way of perceptual reasoning has damaged our world. This has been the means by which emotional reasoning has made an imprint on society. Rationality is truly the general strategy to approach our problems and we need to do so on a basic, daily practice within our individual lives.

In short, concentrate on the conversation so that you can fully appreciate the person that you are in contact with. If not interested, be genuine enough to respectfully state your lack of shared interest without being abusive or intolerant. Don't make it a policy to make any more of things that is actually being expressed and don't read things into the exchanges that are not being expressed or obviously true to a casual observer. If you don't understand or need more information, say so. As an individual or as a society, expect that there must be actual factual evidence to support what is being stated by those who take a portion of your time up with their thoughts or ideas. Don't let someone off the hook by allowing them to spout off without having anything of material support (facts, information, etc.) to provide backup to their personage and verbosity. In short, require those who speak to you have something of value to share-rather than let their "feelings" be their means to gain an audience. (Needing to "vent" seems to have become a human occupation for many-spouting off is now chic). After all, their feelings are no greater or lesser in value than your own-if you want a typically low-value conversation then feelings may be OK. (Not always low-value I admit, but frequently to be the case, or so it seems).

Finally, it is sensible and considerate to reasonably acknowledge that emotion is a part of humanity for a reason, and even though I do not have the exact explanation for its place in our being, it must have importance. Just as I cannot point to the exact purpose for brambles and thistles, they must be of value or our Creator would not have made them a portion of the environment. In some instance, when we lose a loved one or feel great pain and disappointment, it may be all that we can handle the moment. It may be the only thing that will allow us to get through the moment until we can process and consider the instance and circumstance involved. Also, our gut instincts (frequently emotional-based) have been able to save us great injury and suffering thus it is necessary to consider the utility to this unexplained ability to "know" our environment in these instances. I have valued the times when this was able to provide me security and protection. Knowing if, and, when to employ these skills is the truly important thing to understand-not the primary means of interaction with our world, absent reason. However, its use should be novel in its utility, not standard operating procedure for life.

The essential issue involved in this entire treaties and the reason that I have written it is that our present-era, preeminence for emotion over reason as a valued source of understanding, is illogical. Believing based on emotion as reality has, perceptually, altered our world. As it continued, our behavior is frequently a means of ensuring or forwarding our emotional, (feeling-based) self-interest rather than of addressing to the needs of self and others from a rational approach. Unless we consider the fallacy to this emotional strategy, we may doom ourselves to a return to a time of great suffering and lacking for our civilized society as has previously occurred. There was a point in our past history which was entitled "the age of reason." After that point, the follow-up was a sensible consideration for the total sum of self that allowed understanding that emotion has a place also.

This has continued to the present period in our civilized development where we have, in principle, taken our perceptual reality to the opposite end of the spectrum with reason being marginalized in preference for the triad of emotion, feeling, and pleasure-along with subjective reality. As such, the tendency of humanity to behave in an extreme nature from one pole to the other pole (dichotomies) persists and is at its fullest variance as an excess of preference for "feeling good." This will be a source of a future absent the promise and potential which may be realized wherein a balanced approach with a return to the triad of truth, right-wrong, and facts-based on what objective reality will allow.

Great moments in history of civilization have rested on making decisions that were not what one preferred (or made one feel good), but what was essential for all. This represents the greatest example of an honorable, unselfish manner that places reason (and the interests of others) above feeling good or getting one's needs met (or their constituencies needs met). Nothing, by itself, will be the ultimate source our security yet we have strayed from our obvious best interest from a previous time when facts trumped opinions, and truth was more relevant than spin. This is our present state. If we fail to operate with a respect for, and observed need for, reason and the utility of truth, right-wrong dichotomy, and facing our world with keen awareness to our reality absent what we wish it to be-then we will proceed for a time to come. Failure to do so will be detrimental to our future. Something taken absent from its source will not stand.

Conclusion and Summary
What I've Learned

There seems to be a balancing act for Western civilization—at least within the United States—between the lack of faith practiced by some young adults versus the adherence to spiritual and religious principles by a like number of older adults. However, this is not to say that in all, or even many, cases this is the gospel fact, rather, it appears to be so based upon a preponderance of the literature. There are always exceptions, but the following appears apparent:

- The lack of non-evangelical church activity corresponds to the advent of the "me first" principles that were brought to bear with concerns of protecting self-esteem at all costs. This is said because many lessons were sacrificed at the expense of ideals that have led to an entitled attitude by a statistically significant number of those in their teens, 20s, and early 30s. Humility, putting others first, and public service have suffered relative to the population available to provide for those in need. (There may be more involved in community service, but the percentage of those available versus those who are actually involved is less—there are just more people on earth now).

- This idea of giving trophies to everyone who participates suggests to the young person that being successful is not important and that being in the game is all that is important. This provides the false illusion that one will be rewarded with less than the best effort or expertise. This is not indicative of what life is all about, thus the individual approaching adulthood has a rude awakening as to the facts of life with few opportunities experienced when faith and effort were practiced in unison.

- Older Americans serve to counterbalance the lack of otherness that is demonstrated by younger Americans; while younger Americans who grow into middle age "find" spirituality—if not of a Creator-oriented type, then, of a search for why things have not turned out as they felt that they were entitled to expect in their 20s and early 30s.

- Older Americans will be spiritual in main part because those who engage in reckless behaviors do not reach elder status with any great regularity; leaving those who do reach elderly status being those who have lived a safer, healthier (spiritually, physically, and mentally) life.

- People who are spiritual are generally happier and have a greater degree of being well-adjusted to their environment with increased inner strength available to deal with disappointment, thereby avoiding depression and anxiety as compared to those without the benefit of a spiritual lifestyle.

- Spiritual people cope better with life's problems.

- All groups of individuals who demonstrate a spiritual lifestyle also demonstrate greater success than is seen in comparison to those within groups who do not practice the spirituality principles.

- Having a purpose to life leads to more successful goal-directed activities.

- The meaning to life includes a Creator and for those with a traditional spiritual existence, the Creator is at the center of that existence.

- A successful recovery from drugs and alcohol dependency includes having a spiritual awakening.

- Not all spiritual experiences are positive; only when individuals can forgive themselves can they accept that God has already forgiven them.

- All of these generally reliable estimations lead to the conclusion that life will go on as it has with the young lamenting the old and the old lamenting the young as they have since early Roman times (if not even earlier).

Every age would like to see itself as being special in comparison to another age, but it does not appear realistic to ascribe any special legacy to this age over another on the merits of what has been learned by this discourse on spirituality. From one age to another, it appears reasonable to conclude that lessons must be relearned or, at different ages in our lives, we relearn lessons that were understood by those who had come before us. Nevertheless, at the present time, we stand looking to see which side of 50% will take the lead towards our progress or regression as a society. As it stands presently, 50% seems to be a rather accurate approximation of those who practice traditional religion and spirituality versus those secular individuals who are swayed by New Age ideas and concepts that exclude traditional values.

We are either in the beginning of a great falling away from spiritual and religious lifestyles with the coming into population majority of those who do not feel inclined to place a premium on spiritual matters in which obedience to a Creator is involved, or we will right the ship with succeeding generations who feel the error of their parents from this present generation. The great equalizer in this struggle is what was termed by former President Lyndon Johnson as the Silent Majority. They exist in this country as those who practice religious or spiritual lifestyles, going quietly about living day-to-day without fanfare, and providing stability to our country.

With all of this speculation over the demise of spirituality and religious participation, the reality is that there are many young adults who attend church, raise their children in the fear of God, and provide allegiance to Christian ways of living (spirituality included). The real issue to observe is that there is a general polarization between those who believe in a Creator and practice a faith and those who are of the flesh. It is either beer and football on Saturday and Sunday, or church with a family eating together after the service. It is either the idolizing of rock stars, movie stars, or professional athletes, or gaining security and solace with obedience to an omnipotent, sovereign Creator.

One discomforting fact of the present era is the appearance of non-Creator-oriented spirituality practices that seem to be flat and ineffective for the long-term benefits of those practicing them. Exercise and meditation are essential in this increasingly hectic and stressful environment, but without a source of spirituality as is found in the personage of a Creator, there is little permanent support for the person. One goes to and fro without the stability provided by a God of their understanding.

Equally discouraging is the tendency of the present generations to dispose of anything that causes any discomfort or controversy because no one wants to rock the boat or cause even an insect to feel distress. A look at how we are constantly redefining things due to someone stating anger over the way it makes them feel, without accepting that not everyone will be happy no matter what this society does, leads to a conclusion that a form of paranoia exists. This is particularly telling of the way in which spirituality has been diluted to include practically any exercise at the exclusion of mention of a Creator as being central to the experience, lest an atheist or some other minute percentage of the populace be offended.

One can stretch (yoga) and it is called spiritual, one can experiment with hallucination-inducing drugs and it is termed "being spiritual," or one can hug a tree and it is spiritual, but to speak of God or Christ is frowned upon by an increasingly secular number that are quickly becoming the majority. The difference, and a strategic error for those of a spiritual tendency, is that in this culture, the concept of tolerance has allowed secular perspectives to ferment and approach a close approximation to a majority, and that group seems intolerant of those who do have a traditional spiritual basis to their perspective. In the interest of being tolerant, those of traditional religious and spiritual persuasions have unwittingly allowed for the New Age, which speaks of inclusion as a guiding precept while discriminating against those of traditionalist values.

Another tendency of the recent past within society is the need for "new and improved" and the embrace of "change." Somehow, society has determined that if something is new, it is necessarily better than what is presently in use, and that throwing off tradition is to be seen as a necessary change for the better. No one can state that all that has occurred with respect to religion and spirituality practices over the past several centuries is all good and beneficial, but to discard beliefs, practices, and tradition is senseless when nothing of substance is provided to replace it. Instead of discarding those aspects of something that is detrimental and replacing them with adjustments to practices that are beneficial and nurturing, society discards all and starts anew. This is what has occurred with spirituality as the Creator is ignored; and mind, soul, and body are the new and improved way or the flavor of the day.

With all of the talk forecasting the demise of civilization as we know it, there is no certainty to our fate. Even religious texts states that no one knows the hour or the day, save the Creator, so we can only anticipate the next day with the hope that that which ills us will be addressed in a positive manner to ensure that hope, peace, and connectedness continue to allow civilization to endure. The question is, "Who will right the ship?" This appears to be an individual decision, in which the person has to account for their own journey and decide whether a spiritual adventure is worthy of their efforts, energies, and time.

Religion and spirituality, at least at the traditional level, seem to be best served together. The orientation to a Creator and of the precepts and traditions associated with religion bode well as an introduction to the development of a spiritual life. Following this initial presentation of ideals and ideas, the search for a purpose to life and of the meaning for life, are natural follow-up steps to the development of a well-rounded spiritual life. My research has concluded that the two concepts of religion and spirituality are best served as a dual treatment that does not exclude one or the other, but makes best use of each one of these concepts in a complement that develops one and then the other.

Spirituality is positively correlated with physical and mental well-being, allows for coping skills that address adversity effectively, and humbly and realistically places individuals apart from that which can destroy them. However, whether people follow this path depends upon if they can delay their gratification for a future reward, or are concerned about immediate gratification found in material things that will dissolve, decease, or disappear in the future. Seems rather simple, doesn't it not?

About The Author

Dr. Michael A. Gray is a family descendent of English Tudor-era monarchy and of Sir John Locke, physician and philosopher. Locke is considered by some to be the "father of English psychology" with his work provided the initial concepts that led to the formation of psychology-both as a science and a disciple. His concept of "self" has been expanded on throughout the centuries and is a hyphenated conceptual expression of psychology, in action, in our modern world.

Dr. Gray has endeavored, for his part, to utilize over 17+ years of college-based education in various fields of all stages of collegiate-degreed programs (in political science/legal studies, leisure and recreational therapy concentration, and counseling psychology @ multiple degree levels (MSCE and Doctor of Education). This utility of this, and other trainings, is based on a self-felt need to continue the "family business" of psychology as an on-going interest. He uses his college education, occupational trainings, and self-study; as well as long-term mental health service provision to various populations, to consider the human condition.

His work serves to share his concerns regarding psychology of "self" and for the sustainability of humanity. This concern leads to his writings regarding the need for, yet current departure from, a Judeo-Christian spiritual lifestyle. This is his contention as it relates to the secular, humanistic majority of western civilization in the present era. These interests have been served by a primary, additional application of an adult-life personal study of scriptural prose.

Bibliography

Albrecht, N. "Does Meditation Play an Integral Role in Achieving High-level Wellness as Defined by Travis and Ryan (2004)?" *Journal of Complementary and Integrative Medicine* 8, no. 1 (2011): 1–27.

Allen, T., and C. Lo. "Religiosity, Spirituality and Substance Abuse." *Journal of Drug Issues* 40, no. 2 (2010): 433–459.

Baetz, M., and J. Toews. "In Review: Clinical Implications of Research on Religion, Spirituality, and Mental Health." *Canadian Journal of Psychiatry* 54, no. 5 (2009): 292–301.

Ball, D., R. Hampton, A. Chronis, and M. Bunker. "The Development of Spirituality and its Effect on Consumer Behavior." *American Marketing Association Conference Proceedings: 2001* 12 (2001): 3–5.

Baruth, L., and M. Manning. *Multicultural Counseling and Psychotherapy: A Lifetime Perspective, 3rd Ed..* New York: Merrill Prentiss-Hall, 2003.

Beck, Judith S. "Cognitive Therapy: Basics and Beyond," 1975.

Berg, G., R. Crowe, B. Wong, and J. Siebert. "Trends in Publication of Spirituality/Religiosity Articles in Critical Care Populations." *Journal Religious Health* 49 (2010): 333–336.

Bhana, A., and S. Bachoo. "The Determinants of Family Resilience Among Families in Low- and Middle-income Contexts: A Systematic Literature Review." *Psychological Society of South Africa* 41, no. 2 (2011): 131–139.

Blazer, D. "Religion, Spirituality, and Mental Health: What We Know and Why This is a Tough Topic to Research." *The Canadian Journal of Psychiatry* 54, no. 5 (2009): 281–282.

Brown University. "Integrate Spirituality into Substance Abuse Treatment for Sustained Abstinence." *Brown University Digest of Addiction Theory & Application* 18, no. 1 (1999): 1–2.

Brown, A., V. Pavlik, R. Shegog, S. Whitney, L. Friedman, C. Romero, G. C. Davis, I. Cech, T. R. Kosten, and Volk, R. J. "Association of Spirituality and Sobriety During a Behavioral Spirituality Intervention for Twelve Step (TS) Recovery." *The American Journal of Drug and Alcohol Abuse* 33 (2007): 611–617.

Carr, T., S. Hicks-Moore, and P. Montgomery. "What's so Big About the 'Little Things': A Phenomenological Inquiry into the Meaning of Spiritual Care in Dementia." *Dementia* 10 (2011): 399–414.

Cauce, A. "Is Multicultural Psychology A-scientific?: Diverse Methods for Diversity Research." *Cultural Diversity and Ethnic Minority Psychology* 17, no. 3 (2011): 228–233.

Chang-Ho, C., T. Perry, and D. Clarke-Pine. "Considering Personal Religiosity in Adolescent Delinquency: The Role of Depression, Suicidal Ideation, and Church Guideline." *Journal of Psychology and Christianity* 30, no. 1 (2011): 3–15.

Collins, M. (2006). "Religiousness and Spirituality as Possible Recovery Variables in Treated and Natural Recovery." *Alcoholism Treatment Quarterly* 24, no. 4 (2066): 119–135.

Connor, B., M. Anglin, J. Annon, and D. Longshore. "Special Issue: Effects of Religiosity and Spirituality on Drug Treatment Outcomes." *Journal of Behavioral Health Services & Research* 36, no. 2 (2009): 189–198.

Dalrymple, W. (2009). "Spiritual Awakening." *New Statesman Ltd.* 138 (2009): 33.

Dambrun, M., and M. Ricard. "Self-centeredness and Self-lessness: A Theory of Self-based Psychological Functioning and its Consequences for Happiness." *Review of General Psychology* 15, no. 2 (2011): 138–157.

Danbolt, L., P. Moller, L. Lars, and K. Hestad. "The Personal Significance of Religiousness and Spirituality in Patients with Schizophrenia." *International Journal for the Psychology of Religion* 21 (2011): 145–158.

Dein, S. "Religion, Spirituality, and Mental Health: Theoretical and Clinical Perspectives." *Psychiatric Times* 27, no. 1 (2010): 28, 30, 32.

DeKlerk, J., A. Boshoff, and R. Van Wyk. "Spirituality in Practice: Relationships Between Meaning in Life, Commitment, and Motivation." *Journal of Management, Spirituality, & Religion* 3, no. 4 (2010): 319–347.

Denney, R., J. Aten, and K. Leavell. "Posttraumatic Spiritual Growth: A Phenomenological Study of Cancer Survivors." *Mental Health, Religion & Culture* 14, no. 4 (2010): 371–391.

Doswell, W., M. Kouyate, and J. Taylor. "The Role of Spirituality in Preventing Early Sexual Behavior." *American Journal of Health Studies* 18, no. 4 (2003): 195–202.

Ellison, C., and D. Fan. "Daily Spiritual Experiences and Psychological Well-being Among US Adults." *Social Indicators Research* 88 (2008): 247–271.

Faull, K., M. Hills, G. Cochrane, J. Gray, M. Hunt, C. McKenzie, and L. Winter. "Investigation of Health Perspectives of Those with Physical Disabilities: The Role of Spirituality as a Determinant of Health." *Disability and Rehabilitation* 26, no. 3 (2004): 129–144.

Fife, J., H. Sayles, A. Adegoke, J. McCoy, M. Stovall, and C. Verdant. "Religious Typologies and Health Risk Behaviors of African American College Students." *North American Journal of Psychology* 13, no. 2 (2011): 313–330.

Fischer, P., A. Ai, N. Aydin, D. Frey, and S. Haslam. "The Relationship Between Religious Identity and Preferred Coping Strategies: An Examination of the Relative Importance of Interpersonal and Intrapersonal Coping in Muslim and Christian Faiths." *Review of General Psychology* 14, no. 4 (2010): 365–381.

Frankl, V. *Man's Search for Meaning.* (Boston, MA: Beacon Press, 2006).

Galanter, M. "Spirituality and Addiction: A Research and Clinical Perspective." *The American Journal on Addictions* 15 (2006): 286–292.

Gill, C., C. Barrio-Minton, and J. Myers. "Spirituality and Religiosity: Factors Affecting Wellness Among Low-income, Rural Women." *Journal of Counseling & Development* 88 (2010): 293–302.

Goldberg, Y., J. Eastwood, J. Laguardia, and J. Danckert, "Boredom: An Emotional Experience Distinct from Apathy, Anhedonia, or Depression." *Journal of Social and Clinical Psychology* 30, no. 6 (2011): 647–666.

Good, M., T. Willoughby, and M. Busseri. "Stability and Change in Adolescent Spirituality/Religiosity: A Person-centered Approach." *Developmental Psychology* 47, no. 2 (2011): 538–550.

Gray, H., K. Ishii, and N. Ambady. "Misery Loves Company: When Sadness Increases the Desire for Social Connectedness." *Personality and Social Psychology Bulletin,* 37, no. 11 (2011): 1438–1448.

Grouzet, F., T. Kasser, A. Ahuvia, J. Dols, Y. Kim, S. Lau, S., R. Ryan, S. Saunders, P. Schumck, and K. Sheldon. "The Structure of Goal Content Across 15 Cultures." *Journal of Personality and Social Psychology* 89, no. 5 (2005): 800–816.

Guthrie, T., and T. Stickley. "Spiritual Experience and Mental Distress: A Clergy Perspective." *Mental Health, Religion & Culture* 11, no. 4 (2008): 387–402.

Hadzic, M. "Spirituality and Mental Health: Current Research and Future Directions." *Journal of Spirituality in Mental Health* 13, no. 4 (2011): 223–235.

Hardy, S., J. White, Z. Zhang, and J. Ruchty. "Parenting and the Socialization of Religiousness and Spirituality." *Psychology of Religion and Spirituality* 3, no. 3 (2011): 217–230.

Hargrove, L. "Finding Meaning Through Spirituality." *Alberni Valley Times*, October 14, 2011, B4.

Heinz, A., D. Epstein, and K. Preston. "Spiritual/Religious Experiences and In-treatment Outcomes in an Inner-city Program for Heroin and Cocaine Dependence." *Journal of Psychoactive Drugs* 39, no. 1 (2007): 41–49.

Hilbers, J., A. Haynes, and J. Kivikko, "Spirituality and Health: An Exploratory Study of Hospital Patients' Perspectives." *Australian Health Review* 34, no. 1 (2010): 3–10.

Hill, P., and R. Hood. *Measures of Religiosity.* Birmingham, AL: Religious Education Press 1999.

Hitlin, S. "Values as the Core of Personal Identity: Drawing Links Between Two Theories of Self." *Social Psychology Quarterly* 66, no. 2 (2003): 118–137.

Hitlin, S., and J. Pilavin. "Values: Reviving a Dormant Concept." *Annual Review of Sociology* 30, (2004): 359–393.

Holder, M., B. Coleman, and J. Wallace. "Spirituality, Religiousness, and Happiness in Children Aged 8–12 Years." *Journal of Happiness Studies* 11 (2010): 131–150.

Holt, C., M. Shipp, M. Eloubeidi, M. Fouad, K. Britt, and M. Norena. "Your Body is the Temple: Impact of a Spiritually-based Colorectal Cancer Educational Intervention Delivered Through Community Health Advisors." *Health Promotion Practice* 12 (2011): 577–588.

Jarusiewicz, B. "Spirituality and Addiction: Relationship to Recovery and Relapse." *Alcoholism Treatment Quarterly* 18, no. 4 (2000): 99–109.

Johnson, K., J. Tulsky, J. Hays, R. Arnold, M. Olsen, J. Lindquist, and K. Steinhauser. "Which Domains of Spirituality are Associated with Anxiety and Depression in Patients with Advanced Illness." *Journal of General Internal Medicine* 26, no. 7 (2011): 751–758.

Johnson, T., V. Sheets, and J. Kristeller. "Empirical Identification of Dimensions of Religiousness and Spirituality." *Mental Health, Religion & Culture* 11, no. 8 (2008): 745–767.

Kaskutas, L., N. Turk, J. Bond, and C. Weisner. "The Role of Religion, Spirituality and Alcoholics Anonymous in Sustained Sobriety." *Alcoholism Treatment Quarterly* 21, no. 1 (2003), 1–16.

Kim, L. "Improving the Workplace with Spirituality." *The Journal for Quality & Participation,* October 2009, 32–35.

Koenig, H. "Research on Religion, Spirituality, and Mental Health: A Review." *The Canadian Journal of Psychiatry* 54, no. 5 (2009): 283–291.

Korinek, A., and R. Arrendondo. "The Spiritual Health Inventory (SHI): Assessment of an Instrument for Measuring Spiritual Health in a Substance Abusing Population." *Alcoholism Treatment Quarterly* 22, no. 2 (2004): 55–66.

Larson, D., and H. Koenig. "Religion and Mental Health: Evidence for an Association." *International Review of Psychiatry* 13, no. 2 (2001): 67–78.

Larson, D., and S. Larson. "Spirituality's Potential Relevance to Physical and Emotional Health: A Brief Review of Quantitative Research." *Journal of Psychology and Theology* 31, no. 1(2003): 37–51.

Laudet, A. "The Road to Recovery: Where are We Going and How do We Get There? Empirically-driven Conclusions and Future Directions for Service Development and Research." *Substance Use & Misuse* 43 (2008): 2001–2020.

LePage, J., and E. Garcia-Rea. "The Association Between Healthy Lifestyle Behaviors and Relapse Rates in a Homeless Veteran Population." *The American Journal of Drug and Alcohol Abuse* 34 (2008): 171–176.

Lettieri, D., M. Sayers, and H. Pearson, eds. *Theories of Drug Abuse* (NIDA Research Monograph No. 30). Rockville, MD: NIDA, 1980.

Leyden, K., A. Goldberg, and P. Michelbach. "Understanding the Pursuit of Happiness in Ten Major Cities." *Urban Affairs Review* 47 (2011): 861–888.

Longshore, D., M. Anglin, and B. Conner. "Are Religiosity and Spirituality Useful Constructs in Drug Treatment Research?" *Journal of Behavioral Health Services & Research* 36, no. 2 (2008): 177–188.

Lowis, M., A. Edwards, and M. Burton. "Coping with Retirement: Well-being, Health, and Religion." *The Journal of Psychology* 143, no. 4 (2009), 427–448.

MacDonald, D. "Spirituality: Description, Measurement, and Relation to the Five Factor Model of Personality." *Journal of Personality* 68, no. 1 (2000): 153–197.

Magura, S., E. Knight, H. Vogel, D. Mahmood, A. Laudet, and A. Rosenblum. "Mediators of Effectiveness in Dual-focus Self-help Groups." *The American Journal of Drug and Alcohol Abuse* 29, no. 2 (2003): 301–322.

Managan, K. "Medical Schools Begin Teaching Spiritual Side of Health Care." *The Chronicle of Higher Education,* March 7, 1997: http://chronicle.com.archives

Marques, J. "A Spiritual Look at the Recession: This Too Shall Pass." *The Journal of Quality & Participation,* July 2009, 26–29.

Marston, J. "Meaning in Life: A Spiritual Matter—Projected Changes Post-retirement for Baby Boomers." *Journal of Religion, Spirituality & Aging* 22, no. 4 (2010): 329–342.

Martin, M. "Paradoxes of Happiness." *Journal of Happiness Studies* 9 (2008): 171–184.

Mason, S., F. Deane, P. Kelly, and T. Crowe. "Do spirituality and religiosity help in the management of cravings in substance abuse treatment?" *Substance Use and Misuse* 44 (2009): 1926–1940.

Maton, K. "Spirituality, Religion, and Community Psychology: Historical Perspective, Positive Potential, and Challenges." *Journal of Community Psychology* 29, no. 5 (2001): 605–613.

Mauss, I., A. Shallcross, A. Troy, O. John, E. Ferrer, F. Wilhelm, and J. Gross. (2011). "Don't Hide Your Happiness! Positive Emotion Dissociation, Social Connectedness, and Psychological Functioning." *Journal of Personality and Social Psychology* 31, January 2011, 1–11.

May, W. "Spiritual Focus as a Therapeutic Strategy." *Behavioral Health Management,* 14, no. 5 (1994): 35–37.

McGovern, T., and B. Benda. "Themes and Patterns of Spirituality-religiousness and Alcohol/Other Drug Problems." *Alcoholism Treatment Quarterly* 24, no. 1-2 (2006): 1–5.

McMinn, M., W. Hathaway, S. Woods, and K. Snow. (2009). "What American Psychological Association Leaders Have to Say About Psychology of Religion and Spirituality." *Psychology of Religion and Spirituality* 1, no. 1 (2009): 3–13.

Miller, D. "Programs in Social Work Embrace the Teachings of Spirituality." *The Chronicle of Higher Education,* The Faculty Page: A12, May 18, 2001.

Miller, W., and E. Kurtz. "Models of Alcoholism Used in Treatment: Contrasting AA and Other Perspectives with which it is Often Confused." *Journal of Studies on Alcohol* 55 (1994): 159–166.

Miller, W., and M. Bogenschutz. "Spirituality and Addiction." *Southern Medical Journal* 100, no. 4 (2007): 433–436.

Mohatt, N., C. Fok, R. Burket, D. Henry, and J. Allen. (2011). "Assessment of Awareness of Connectedness as a Culturally-based Protective Factor for Alaska Native Youth." *Cultural Diversity and Ethnic Minority Psychology* 17, no. 4 (2011): 444–455.

Molzahn, A., and L. Sheilds. "Why is it so Hard to Talk About Spirituality?" *The Canadian Nurse* 104, no. 1 (2008): 25–29.

Munro, E. "Spiritual Awakening." *Therapy Today* 21, no. 4 (2010): 8.

Nasim, A., S. Utsey, R. Corona, and F. Belgrave. "Religiosity, Refusal Efficacy, and Substance Use Among African-American Adolescents and Young Adults." *Journal of Ethnicity in Substance Abuse* 5, no. 3 (2006): 29–49.

Neff, J., and S. MacMasters. "Applying Behavior Change Models to Understand Spiritual Mechanisms Underlying Change in Substance Abuse Treatment." *The American Journal of Drug and Alcohol Abuse* 31 (2005): 669–684.

New World Communication. "Vatican Issues New Age Warning: Calls Trend in Spirituality no Substitute for Christian Faith." *Washington Times,* February 4, 2003.

Newberg, A., and M. Waldman. *How God Changes Your Brain: Breakthrough Findings from a Leading Neuroscientist.* New York, NY: Random House, 2010.

Nichols, L., and B. Hunt. "The Significance of Spirituality for Individuals with Chronic Illness: Implications for Mental Health Counseling." *Journal of Mental Health Counseling* 33, no. 1 (2011): 51–66.

Nugent, R. "What Does Spiritual But Not Religious Really Mean?" *York Daily Record,* Viewpoints, 1, October, 2011.

O'Connell, K., and S. Skevington. Spiritual, Religious, and Personal Beliefs are Important and Distinctive to Assessing Quality of Life in Health: A Comparison of Theoretical Models, *British Journal of Health Psychology* 15 (2010): 729–748.

Pepper, M., T. Jackson, and D. Uzzell. "A Study of Multidimensional Religion Constructs and Values in the United Kingdom." *Journal for the Scientific Study of Religion* 49, no. 1 (2010): 127–146.

Piderman, K., T. Schneekloth, S. Pankratz, S. Maloney, and S. Altchuler. "Spirituality in Alcoholics During Treatment. *The American Journal on Addictions* 16 (2007): 232–237.

Plante, T., and D. Pardini. "Religious Denomination Affiliation and Psychological Health: Results From a Substance Abuse Population." Paper presented at the annual meeting of the American Psychological Association, Washington: DC., August, 2000.

Potts, M. "The End of Materialism: How Evidence of the Paranormal is Bringing Science and Spirit Together." *The Journal of Parapsychology* 74, no. 1 (2010): 173–178.

Powell, L., L. Shahabi, and C. Thoresen. "Religion and Spirituality: Linkage to Physical Health." *American Psychologist* 58, no. 1 (2003): 36–52.

Redman, D. "Stressful Life Experiences and the Roles of Spirituality Among People with a History of Substance Abuse and Incarceration." *Journal of Religion Spirituality in Social Work: Social Thought* 27, no. 1-2 (2008): 47–67.

Ribaudo, A., and M. Takahashi. "Temporal Trends in Spirituality Research: A Meta-analysis of Journal Abstracts between 1944 and 2003." *Journal of Religion, Spirituality & Aging* 20, no. 1-2 (2008): 16–28.

Rican, P., and P. Janosova. "Spirituality as a Basic Aspect of Personality: A Cross-cultural Verification of Piedmont's Model." *The International Journal for the Psychology of Religion* 20 (2010): 2–13.

Rippentrop, A., E. Altmaier, J. Chen, E. Found, and V. Keffala. "The Relationship Between Religion/Spirituality and Physical Health, Mental Health, and Pain in a Chronic Pain Population." *Pain* 116 (2005): 311–321.

Roemer, M. "Religion and Psychological Distress in Japan." *Social Forces* 89, no. 2 (2010): 559–583.

Rowan, N., A. Faul, R. Cloud, and R. Huber. "The Higher Power Relationship Scale: A Validation." *Journal of Social Work Practice in the Addictions* 6, no. 3 (2006): 81–95.

Ronel, N. "The Experience of Spiritual Intelligence." *The Journal of Transpersonal Psychology* 40, no. 1 (2008): 100–119.

Ruddock, B., and R. Cameron. "Spirituality in Children and Young People: A Suitable Topic for Educational and Child Psychologist? *Educational Psychology in Practice* 26, no. 1 (2010): 25–34.

Sandage, S., and M. Harden. "Relational Spirituality, Differentiation of Self, and Virtue as Predictors of Intercultural Development." *Mental Health, Religion & Culture* 14, no. 8 (2011): 819–838.

Saroglou, V. "Believing, Bonding, Behaving, and Belonging: The Big Four Religious Dimensions and Cultural Variation." *Journal of Cross-Cultural Psychology* 42, no. 8 (2011): 1320–1340.

Saroglou, V., and A. Cohen. "Psychology of Culture and Religion: Introduction to the JCCP Special Edition." *Journal of Cross-Cultural Psychology* 42, no. 8 (2011): 1309–1319.

S. Schwartz. "Universals in the Content and Structure of Values: Theoretical Advances and Empirical Tests in Twenty Countries," In *Advances in Experimental Social Psychology,* Vol. 25, edited by M. Zanna, 1–65. Orlando FL: Academic Press, 1992.

Shorkey, C., M. Uebel, and L. Windsor. "Measuring Dimensions of Spirituality in Chemical Dependence Treatment and Recovery: Research and Practice." *International Journal of Mental Health Addiction* 6 (2008): 286–305.

Simpson, D., E. Woike, A. Musick, J. Newman, and D. Fuqua. "The Relationship of Religious Participation to Relationship with God." *Journal of Psychology and Christianity* 28, no. 4 (2009): 360–369.

Slife, B., and M. Whoolery. "Are Psychology's Main Methods Biased Against the Worldview of Many Religious People?" *Journal of Psychology and Theology* 34, no. 3 (2006): 217–231.

Sointu, E., and L. Woodhead. "Spirituality, Gender, and Expressive Selfhood." *Journal for the Scientific Study of Religion* 47, no. 2 (2008): 259–276.

Speckhardt, R. "Finding Faith in Humankind." *The Futurist,* March-April (2010): 37–38.

Springer, R. "America Needs a Spiritual Awakening," Editorial, *Peoria Journal Star,* February 5, 2010.

Stanley, M., A. Bush, M. Camp, J. Jameson, L. Phillips, C. Barber, D. Zeno, J. Lomax, J. Cully, "Older Adults' Preferences for Religion/

Spirituality in Treatment for Anxiety and Depression." *Aging & Mental Health* 15, no. 3 (2011): 334–343.

Stanton, A., J. Bower, and C. Low. "Posttraumatic Growth After Cancer," In *Handbook of Posttraumatic Growth: Research and Practice*, edited by L.G. Calhoun and R.G. Tedeschi, 138–178. Mahwah NJ: Erlbaum, 2006.

Stewart, C. "Client Spirituality and Substance Abuse Treatment Outcomes." *Journal of Religion & Spirituality in Social Work: Social Thought* 27, no. 4 (2008): 385–404.

Stewart, C., G. Kieske, and J. Pringle. "Religiosity as a Predictor of Successful Post-treatment Abstinence for African-American Clients." *Journal of Social Work Practice in the Addictions* 7, no. 4 (2007): 75–92.

Stillman, T., F. Fincham, K. Vohs, N. Lambert, and C. Phillips. "The Material and Immaterial in Conflict: Spirituality Reduces Conspicuous Consumption." *Journal of Economic Psychology* 33 (2012): 1–7.

Straughn, J., and S. Feld. "America as a 'Christian Nation?' Understanding Religious Boundaries of National Identity in the United States." *Sociology of Religion* 71, no. 3 (2010): 280–306.

Tovar-Murray, D. "The Multiple Determinants of Religious Behaviors and Spiritual Beliefs on Well-being." *Journal of Spirituality in Mental Health* 13, no. 3 (2011): 182–192.

Twenge, J., and W. Campbell. *The Narcissism Epidemic: Living in the Age of Entitlement*, New York, NY: Simon & Schulster, 2010.

Vaillant, G. "Alcoholics Anonymous: Cult or Cure?" *Australian and New Zealand Journal of Psychiatry* 39 (2005): 431–436.

Vaillant, G. "Positive Emotions, Spirituality, and the Practice of Psychiatry." *Medicine, Mental Health, Science, Religion, and Well-Being* 6 (2008): 48–62.

Vasegh, S. "Cognitive Therapy of Religious Depressed Patients: Common Concepts Between Christianity and Islam." *Journal of Cognitive Psychotherapy: An International Quarterly* 25, no. 3 (2011): 177–188.

Waldron-Perrine, B., L. Rapport, R. Hanks, M. Lumley, S. Meachen, and P. Hubbarth. "Religion and Spirituality in Rehabilitation

Outcomes Among Individuals with Traumatic Brain Injury."
Rehabilitation Psychology 56, no. 2 (2011): 107–116.

Walsh, R. "Lifestyle and Mental Health." *American Psychologist* 66, no.
7 (2011): 579–592.

Weaver, A., K. Pargament, K. Flannelly, and J. Oppenheimer. "Trends
in the Scientific Study of Religion, Spirituality, and Health: 1965–
2000." *Journal of Religion and Health* 45, no. 2 (2006): 208–214.

Wills, E. "Spirituality and Subjective Well-being: Evidences for a New
Domain in the Personal Well-Being Index." *Journal of Happiness
Studies* 10 (2009): 49–69.

Windsor, L., and C. Shorkey. Spiritual Change in Drug Treatment:
Utility of the Christian Inventory of Spirituality." *Substance Abuse*
31, no. 3 (2011): 136–145.

Wink, P., and M. Dillon. "Religiousness, Spirituality, and Psychosocial
Functioning in Late Adulthood: Findings from a Longitudinal
Study." *Psychology of Religion and Spirituality* 5, no. 1 (2008):
102–115.

Yoon, E., J. Hacker, A. Hewitt, M. Abrams, and S. Cleary. "Social
Connectedness, Discrimination, and Social Status as Mediators
of Acculturation/Enculturation and Well-being." *Journal of
Counseling Psychology* (forthcoming), advance online publication,
05 September 2011.

Zaidman, N., and O. Goldstein-Gidoni. "Spirituality as a Discarded
Form of Organizational Wisdom: Field-based Analysis." *Group &
Organizational Management* 36, no. 5 (2011): 630–653.

Zemore, S., and L. Kaskutas. "12-Step Involvement and Peer Helping
in Day Hospital and Residential Programs." *Substance Use & Misuse*
43 (2008): 1882–1903.

Zinnbauer, B., K. Pargament, and A. Scott. "The Emerging Meanings
of Religiousness and Spirituality: Problems and Prospects." *Journal
of Personality* 67, no. 6 (1999): 889–919.

Notes

Notes: Chapter One

[1] A. Nasim et al., "Religiosity, Refusal Efficacy, and Substance Use Among African-American Adolescents and Young Adults," *Journal of Ethnicity in Substance Abuse* 5, no. 3 (2006): 29–49. See also, Piderman et al., "Spirituality in Alcoholics During Treatment, *The American Journal on Addictions* 16 (2007): 232–237.

[2] K. Piderman et al., "Spirituality in Alcoholics," 232.

[3] B. Jarusiewicz, "Spirituality and Addiction: Relationship to Recovery and Relapse." *Alcoholism Treatment Quarterly* 18, no. 4 (2000): 100.

[4] V. Saroglou and A. Cohen, "Psychology of Culture and Religion: Introduction to the JCCP Special Edition," *Journal of Cross-Cultural Psychology* 42, no. 8 (2011): 1309–1319.

[5] C. Chang-Ho, T. Perry, and D. Clarke-Pine, "Considering Personal Religiosity in Adolescent Delinquency: The Role of Depression, Suicidal Ideation, and Church Guideline," *Journal of Psychology and Christianity* 30, no. 1 (2011): 3–15.

[6] For example, see L. Kim, "Improving the Workplace with Spirituality," *The Journal for Quality & Participation,* October 2009, 32–35.

[7] V. Saroglou, "Believing, Bonding, Behaving, and Belonging: The Big Four Religious Dimensions and Cultural Variation," *Journal of Cross-Cultural Psychology* 42, no. 8 (2011): 1320–1340.

[8] L. Hargrove, "Finding Meaning Through Spirituality," *Alberni Valley Times*, October 14, 2011, B4.

[9] M. Hadzic, "Spirituality and Mental Health: Current Research and Future Directions," *Journal of Spirituality in Mental Health* 13, no. 4 (2011): 223–235.

[10] R. Nugent, "What Does Spiritual But Not Religious Really Mean?" *York Daily Record*, Viewpoints, 1, October 2011.

Notes: Chapter Two
[11] C. Shorkey, M. Uebel, and L. Windsor, "Measuring Dimensions of Spirituality in Chemical Dependence Treatment and Recovery: Research and Practice," *International Journal of Mental Health Addiction* 6 (2008): 286–305.

[12] T. Johnson, V. Sheets, and J. Kristeller, "Empirical Identification of Dimensions of Religiousness and Spirituality," *Mental Health, Religion & Culture* 11, no. 8 (2008): 745.

[13] G. Vaillant, "Positive Emotions, Spirituality, and the Practice of Psychiatry," *Medicine, Mental Health, Science, Religion, and Well-Being* 6 (2008): 48.

[14] C. Ellison and D. Fan, "Daily Spiritual Experiences and Psychological Well-being Among US Adults," *Social Indicators Research* 88 (2008): 247–271.

[15] A. Heinz, D. Epstein, and K. Preston, "Spiritual/Religious Experiences and In-treatment Outcomes in an Inner-city Program for Heroin and Cocaine Dependence," *Journal of Psychoactive Drugs* 39, no. 1 (2007): 41–49.

[16] J. Neff and S. MacMasters, "Applying Behavior Change Models to Understand Spiritual Mechanisms Underlying Change in Substance Abuse Treatment," *The American Journal of Drug and Alcohol Abuse* 31 (2005): 669–684.

[17] C. Stewart, G. Kieske, and J. Pringle, "Religiosity as a Predictor of Successful Post-treatment Abstinence for African-American Clients," *Journal of Social Work Practice in the Addictions* 7, no. 4 (2007): 75–92.

[18] Kendler, as cited in Johnson, Sheets, and Kristeller, "Empirical Identification."

[19] Kim, "Improving the Workplace."

[20] M. Pepper, T. Jackson, and D. Uzzell, "A Study of Multidimensional Religion Constructs and Values in the United Kingdom," *Journal for the Scientific Study of Religion* 49, no. 1 (2010): 127–146.

[21] E. Wills, "Spirituality and Subjective Well-being: Evidences for a New Domain in the Personal Well-Being Index," *Journal of Happiness Studies* 10 (2009): 49–69.

[22] Wills, "Spirituality and Subjective Well-being," 52.

[23] P. Rican and P. Janosova, "Spirituality as a Basic Aspect of Personality: A Cross-cultural Verification of Piedmont's Model," *The International Journal for the Psychology of Religion* 20 (2010): 2–13.

[24] At least this is so, according to Y. Goldberg et al., "Boredom: An Emotional Experience Distinct from Apathy, Anhedonia, or Depression," *Journal of Social and Clinical Psychology* 30, no. 6 (2011): 647–666.

[25] P. Hill and R. Hood, *Measures of Religiosity* (Birmingham, AL: Religious Education Press, 1999).

[26] Gorsuch, as cited in Johnson, Sheets, & Kristeller, "Empirical Identification," 745.

[27] Shorkey, Uebel, and Windsor, "Measuring Dimensions."

[28] Shorkey, Uebel, and Windsor, "Measuring Dimensions 292–295.

[29] N. Rowan, A. Faul, R. Cloud, and R. Huber, "The Higher Power Relationship Scale: A Validation," *Journal of Social Work Practice in the Addictions* 6, no. 3 (2006): 81–95.

[30] A. Korinek and R. Arrendondo, "The Spiritual Health Inventory (SHI): Assessment of an Instrument for Measuring Spiritual Health in a Substance Abusing Population," *Alcoholism Treatment Quarterly* 22, no. 2 (2004): 55–66.

[31] Shorkey, Uebel, and Windsor, "Measuring Dimensions."

[32] E. Wills, "Spirituality and Subjective Well-being: Evidences for a New Domain in the Personal Well-Being Index," *Journal of Happiness Studies* 10 (2009): 49–69.

[33] D. MacDonald, "Spirituality: Description, Measurement, and Relation to the Five Factor Model of Personality," *Journal of Personality* 68, no. 1 (2000): 153–197.

Notes: Chapter Three

[34] G. Vaillant, "Alcoholics Anonymous: Cult or Cure?" *Australian and New Zealand Journal of Psychiatry* 39 (2005): 431–436.

[35] S. Mason et al., "Do spirituality and religiosity help in the management of cravings in substance abuse treatment?" *Substance Use and Misuse* 44 (2009): 1926–1940.

[36] A. Laudet, "The Road to Recovery: Where are We Going and How do We Get There? Empirically-driven Conclusions and Future Directions

for Service Development and Research," *Substance Use & Misuse* 43 (2008): 2001–2020.

[37] Fiorentine and Hillhouse, as cited in M. Collins, "Religiousness and Spirituality as Possible Recovery Variables in Treated and Natural Recovery," *Alcoholism Treatment Quarterly* 24, no. 4 (2066): 121.

[38] C. Stewart, "Client Spirituality and Substance Abuse Treatment Outcomes," *Journal of Religion & Spirituality in Social Work: Social Thought* 27, no. 4 (2008): 385–404.

[39] Alcoholics Anonymous, *Twelve Steps and Twelve Traditions* (New York, NY: AA World Services, Inc., 2005): 5–8.

[40] L. Kaskutas et al., "The Role of Religion, Spirituality and Alcoholics Anonymous in Sustained Sobriety," *Alcoholism Treatment Quarterly* 21, no. 1 (2003), 1–16.

[41] Vaillant, "Alcoholics Anonymous: Cult or Cure?" 433

[42] As cited in Vaillant, "Alcoholics Anonymous: Cult or Cure?"

[43] A. Brown, "Association of Spirituality and Sobriety During a Behavioral Spirituality Intervention for Twelve Step (TS) Recovery," *The American Journal of Drug and Alcohol Abuse* 33 (2007): 611–617.

[44] S. Zemore and L. Kaskutas, "12-Step Involvement and Peer Helping in Day Hospital and Residential Programs," *Substance Use & Misuse* 43 (2008): 1882–1903.

[45] Stewart, Kieske, & Pringle, "Religiosity as a Predictor."

[46] W. Miller and M. Bogenschutz, "Spirituality and Addiction," *Southern Medical Journal* 100, no. 4 (2007): 433.

[47] S. Magura et al., "Mediators of Effectiveness in Dual-focus Self-help Groups," *The American Journal of Drug and Alcohol Abuse* 29, no. 2 (2003): 301–322.

[48] Neff and MacMasters, "Applying Behavior Change Models," 670.

[49] D. Redman, "Stressful Life Experiences and the Roles of Spirituality Among People with a History of Substance Abuse and Incarceration," *Journal of Religion Spirituality in Social Work: Social Thought* 27, no. 1-2 (2008): 58

[50] T. McGovern and B. Benda, "Themes and Patterns of Spirituality-religiousness and Alcohol/Other Drug Problems," *Alcoholism Treatment Quarterly* 24, no. 1-2 (2006): 1–5.

[51] B. Connor et al. "Special Issue: Effects of Religiosity and Spirituality on Drug Treatment Outcomes." *Journal of Behavioral Health Services & Research* 36, no. 2 (2009): 189–198.

[52] T. Allen and C. Lo. "Religiosity, Spirituality and Substance Abuse." *Journal of Drug Issues* 40, no. 2 (2010): 433–459.

[53] M. Galanter, "Spirituality and Addiction: A Research and Clinical Perspective," *The American Journal on Addictions* 15 (2006): 286–292. Galanter suggested that spirituality must be considered as one of many alternative methods of treatment.

[54] D. Longshore, M. Anglin, and B. Conner, "Are Religiosity and Spirituality Useful Constructs in Drug Treatment Research?" *Journal of Behavioral Health Services & Research* 36, no. 2 (2008): 177–188.

[55] D. Lettieri, M. Sayers, and H. Pearson, eds., *Theories of Drug Abuse* (NIDA Research Monograph No. 30) (Rockville, MD: NIDA, 1980).

[56] Brown University, "Integrate Spirituality into Substance Abuse Treatment for Sustained Abstinence," *Brown University Digest of Addiction Theory & Application* 18, no. 1 (1999): 1.

[57] W. May, "Spiritual Focus as a Therapeutic Strategy," *Behavioral Health Management,* 14, no. 5 (1994): 36.

[58] Kaskutas et al., "The Role of Religion."

[59] E. Munro, "Spiritual Awakening," *Therapy Today* 21, no. 4 (2010): 8.

Notes: Chapter Four

[60] Ellison and Fan, "Daily Spiritual Experiences"; Miller and Borgenschutz, "Spirituality and Addiction."

[61] T. Guthrie and T. Stickley, "Spiritual Experience and Mental Distress: A Clergy Perspective," *Mental Health, Religion & Culture* 11, no. 4 (2008): 387–402.

[62] J. LePage and E. Garcia-Rea, "The Association Between Healthy Lifestyle Behaviors and Relapse Rates in a Homeless Veteran Population," *The American Journal of Drug and Alcohol Abuse* 34 (2008): 171–176.

[63] T. Plante and D. Pardini, "Religious Denomination Affiliation and Psychological Health: Results From a Substance Abuse Population," Paper presented at the annual meeting of the American Psychological Association, Washington: DC., August, 2000: 1.

[64] H. Koenig, "Research on Religion, Spirituality, and Mental Health: A Review," *The Canadian Journal of Psychiatry* 54, no. 5 (2009): 283.

[65] Koenig, "Research on Religion."

[66] Or so it is suggested by J. Marques, "A Spiritual Look at the Recession: This Too Shall Pass," *The Journal of Quality & Participation*, July 2009, 26–29.

[67] Marques, "A Spiritual Look," 28.

[68] K. Johnson et al., "Which Domains of Spirituality are Associated with Anxiety and Depression in Patients with Advanced Illness?" *Journal of General Internal Medicine* 26, no. 7 (2011): 751–758.

[69] M. Stanley et al., "Older Adults' Preferences for Religion/Spirituality in Treatment for Anxiety and Depression," *Aging & Mental Health* 15, no. 3 (2011): 334–343.

[70] A. Newberg and M. Waldman, *How God Changes Your Brain: Breakthrough Findings from a Leading Neuroscientist* (New York, NY: Random House, 2010).

[71] S. Vasegh, "Cognitive Therapy of Religious Depressed Patients: Common Concepts Between Christianity and Islam," *Journal of Cognitive Psychotherapy: An International Quarterly* 25, no. 3 (2011): 177–188.

[72] L. Danbolt et al., "The Personal Significance of Religiousness and Spirituality in Patients with Schizophrenia," *International Journal for the Psychology of Religion* 21 (2011): 145–158.

[73] A. Newberg and M. Waldman. *How God Changes Your Brain: Breakthrough Findings from a Leading Neuroscientist* (New York, NY: Random House, 2010).

[74] M. Baetz and J. Toews, "In Review: Clinical Implications of Research on Religion, Spirituality, and Mental Health," *Canadian Journal of Psychiatry* 54, no. 5 (2009): 292–301.

[75] A. Stanton, J. Bower, and C. Low, "Posttraumatic Growth After Cancer," In *Handbook of Posttraumatic Growth: Research and Practice,* ed. L.G. Calhoun and R.G. Tedeschi (Mahwah NJ: Erlbaum, 2006): 138-178.

[76] R. Denney, J. Aten, and K. Leavell, "Posttraumatic Spiritual Growth: A Phenomenological Study of Cancer Survivors," *Mental Health, Religion & Culture* 14, no. 4 (2010): 371–391.

[77] C. Holt et al., "Your Body is the Temple: Impact of a Spiritually-based Colorectal Cancer Educational Intervention Delivered Through Community Health Advisors," *Health Promotion Practice* 12 (2011): 577–588.

[78] B. Waldron-Perrine et al., "Religion and Spirituality in Rehabilitation Outcomes Among Individuals with Traumatic Brain Injury," *Rehabilitation Psychology* 56, no. 2 (2011): 107–116.

[79] T. Carr, S. Hicks-Moore, and P. Montgomery, "What's so Big About the 'Little Things?': A Phenomenological Inquiry into the Meaning of Spiritual Care in Dementia," *Dementia* 10 (2011): 399–414.

[80] J. Hilbers, A. Haynes, and J. Kivikko, "Spirituality and Health: An Exploratory Study of Hospital Patients' Perspectives," *Australian Health Review* 34, no. 1 (2010): 3–10.

[81] L. Nichols and B. Hunt, "The Significance of Spirituality for Individuals with Chronic Illness: Implications for Mental Health Counseling," *Journal of Mental Health Counseling* 33, no. 1 (2011): 51–66.

[82] A. Rippentrop et al., "The Relationship Between Religion/Spirituality and Physical Health, Mental Health, and Pain in a Chronic Pain Population," *Pain* 116 (2005): 311–321.

[83] A. Rippentrop et al., "The Relationship Between Religion/Spirituality and Physical Health," 319.

[84] K. Faull et al., "Investigation of Health Perspectives of Those with Physical Disabilities: The Role of Spirituality as a Determinant of Health," *Disability and Rehabilitation* 26, no. 3 (2004): 129–144.

[85] D. Larson and S. Larson, "Spirituality's Potential Relevance to Physical and Emotional Health: A Brief Review of Quantitative Research," *Journal of Psychology and Theology* 31, no. 1(2003): 37–51.

[86] L. Powell, L. Shahabi, and C. Thoresen, "Religion and Spirituality: Linkage to Physical Health," *American Psychologist* 58, no. 1 (2003): 36–52.

Notes: Chapter Five
[87]K. O'Connell and S. Skevington, "Spiritual, Religious, and Personal Beliefs are Important and Distinctive to Assessing Quality of Life in Health: A Comparison of Theoretical Models," *British Journal of Health Psychology* 15 (2010): 729–748.

[88] O'Connell and Skevington, "Spiritual, Religious, and Personal Beliefs," 740.

[89] A. Weaver et al., "Trends in the Scientific Study of Religion, Spirituality, and Health: 1965–2000." *Journal of Religion and Health* 45, no. 2 (2006): 208–214.

[90] A. Ribaudo and M. Takahashi, "Temporal Trends in Spirituality Research: A Meta-analysis of Journal Abstracts between 1944 and 2003," *Journal of Religion, Spirituality & Aging* 20, no. 1-2 (2008): 16–28.

[91] "Vatican Issues New Age Warning: Calls Trend in Spirituality no Substitute for Christian Faith," *Washington Times,* February 4, 2003.

[92] M. McMinn et al., "What American Psychological Association Leaders Have to Say About Psychology of Religion and Spirituality," *Psychology of Religion and Spirituality* 1, no. 1 (2009): 3–13.

[93] D. Larson and H. Koenig, "Religion and Mental Health: Evidence for an Association," *International Review of Psychiatry* 13, no. 2 (2001): 67–78.

[94] M. McMinn et al., "What American Psychological Association Leaders Have to Say About Psychology of Religion and Spirituality," *Psychology of Religion and Spirituality* 1, no. 1 (2009): 3–13.

[95] G. Berg et al., "Trends in Publication of Spirituality/Religiosity Articles in Critical Care Populations," *Journal Religious Health* 49 (2010): 333–336.

[96] A. Molzahn and L. Sheilds, "Why is it so Hard to Talk About Spirituality?" *The Canadian Nurse* 104, no. 1 (2008): 25–29.

[97] L. Windsor and C. Shorkey, Spiritual Change in Drug Treatment: Utility of the Christian Inventory of Spirituality," *Substance Abuse* 31, no. 3 (2011): 136–145.

[98] B. Slife and M. Whoolery, "Are Psychology's Main Methods Biased Against the Worldview of Many Religious People?" *Journal of Psychology and Theology* 34, no. 3 (2006): 217–231.

[99] Slife and Whoolery, "Are Psychology's Main Methods Biased," 219.

[100] R. Speckhardt, "Finding Faith in Humankind," *The Futurist,* March-April (2010): 38.

[101] E. Sointu and L. Woodhead, "Spirituality, Gender, and Expressive Selfhood." *Journal for the Scientific Study of Religion* 47, no. 2 (2008): 259–276.

[102] M. Dambrun and M. Ricard, "Self-centeredness and Self-lessness: A Theory of Self-based Psychological Functioning and its Consequences for Happiness," *Review of General Psychology* 15, no. 2 (2011): 138–157.

[103] J. Twenge and W. Campbell, *The Narcissism Epidemic: Living in the Age of Entitlement* (New York, NY: Simon & Schulster, 2010).

[104] M. Potts, "The End of Materialism: How Evidence of the Paranormal is Bringing Science and Spirit Together," *The Journal of Parapsychology* 74, no. 1 (2010): 173–178.

[105] F. Grouzet et al., "The Structure of Goal Content Across 15 Cultures," *Journal of Personality and Social Psychology* 89, no. 5 (2005): 800–816.

[106] S. Schwartz, "Universals in the Content and Structure of Values: Theoretical Advances and Empirical Tests in Twenty Countries," In *Advances in Experimental Social Psychology*, ed. M. Zanna (Orlando FL: Academic Press, 1992): 25: 1–65.

[107] T. Stillman et al., "The Material and Immaterial in Conflict: Spirituality Reduces Conspicuous Consumption," *Journal of Economic Psychology* 33 (2012): 1–7.

[108] Baetz and Toews, "In Review: Clinical Implications," 295.

[109] L. Baruth and M. Manning, *Multicultural Counseling and Psychotherapy: A Lifetime Perspective* (New York: Merrill Prentiss-Hall, 2003).

[110] S. Sandage and M. Harden, "Relational Spirituality, Differentiation of Self, and Virtue as Predictors of Intercultural Development," *Mental Health, Religion & Culture* 14, no. 8 (2011): 819–838.

[111] A. Cauce, "Is Multicultural Psychology A-scientific?: Diverse Methods for Diversity Research," *Cultural Diversity and Ethnic Minority Psychology* 17, no. 3 (2011): 228–233.

[112] N. Ronel, "The Experience of Spiritual Intelligence," *The Journal of Transpersonal Psychology* 40, no. 1 (2008): 102.

[113] Ronel, "The Experience of Spiritual Intelligence," 103.

[114] P. Wink and M. Dillon, "Religiousness, Spirituality, and Psychosocial Functioning in Late Adulthood: Findings from a Longitudinal Study," *Psychology of Religion and Spirituality* 5, no. 1 (2008): 112.

Notes: Chapter Six

[115] B. Zinnbauer, K. Pargament, and A. Scott, "The Emerging Meanings of Religiousness and Spirituality: Problems and Prospects," *Journal of Personality* 67, no. 6 (1999): 889–919.

[116] R. Nugent, "What Does Spiritual But Not Religious Really Mean?"

[117] J. Straughn and S. Feld, "America as a 'Christian Nation?' Understanding Religious Boundaries of National Identity in the United States," *Sociology of Religion* 71, no. 3 (2010): 280–306.

[118] K. Managan, "Medical Schools Begin Teaching Spiritual Side of Health Care," *The Chronicle of Higher Education,* March 7, 1997.

[119] D. Miller, "Programs in Social Work Embrace the Teachings of Spirituality," *The Chronicle of Higher Education,* The Faculty Page: A12, May 18, 2001.

[120] S. Dein, "Religion, Spirituality, and Mental Health: Theoretical and Clinical Perspectives," *Psychiatric Times* 27, no. 1 (2010): 28, 30, 32.

[121] Nichols and Hunt, "The Significance of Spirituality"

[122] C. Gill, C. Barrio-Minton, and J. Myers, "Spirituality and Religiosity: Factors Affecting Wellness Among Low-income, Rural Women," *Journal of Counseling & Development* 88 (2010): 293–302.

[123] Chang-Ho, Perry, and Clarke-Pine, "Considering Personal Religiosity," 3.

[124] "Youth Define Spirituality in Terms of Positive Behaviors, Connections." *Targeted News Service,* June 21, 2010.

[125] M. Holder, B. Coleman, and J. Wallace, "Spirituality, Religiousness, and Happiness in Children Aged 8–12 Years," *Journal of Happiness Studies* 11 (2010): 131–150; B. Ruddock and R. Cameron, "Spirituality in Children and Young People: A Suitable Topic for Educational and Child Psychologist? *Educational Psychology in Practice* 26, no. 1 (2010): 25–34.

[126] Ruddock and Cameron, "Spirituality in Children," 29.

[127] M. Good, T. Willoughby, and M. Busseri, "Stability and Change in Adolescent Spirituality/Religiosity: A Person-centered Approach," *Developmental Psychology* 47, no. 2 (2011): 538–550.

[128] S. Hardy et al., "Parenting and the Socialization of Religiousness and Spirituality," *Psychology of Religion and Spirituality* 3, no. 3 (2011): 217–230.

[129] J. Fife et al., "Religious Typologies and Health Risk Behaviors of African American College Students," *North American Journal of Psychology* 13, no. 2 (2011): 313–330.

[130] A. Bhana and S. Bachoo, "The Determinants of Family Resilience Among Families in Low- and Middle-income Contexts: A Systematic Literature Review," *Psychological Society of South Africa* 41, no. 2 (2011): 133.

[131] K. Maton, "Spirituality, Religion, and Community Psychology: Historical Perspective, Positive Potential, and Challenges," *Journal of Community Psychology* 29, no. 5 (2001): 605–613.

[132] Maton, "Spirituality, Religion, and Community Psychology."

[133] P. Fischer et al., "The Relationship Between Religious Identity and Preferred Coping Strategies: An Examination of the Relative Importance of Interpersonal and Intrapersonal Coping in Muslim and Christian Faiths," *Review of General Psychology* 14, no. 4 (2010): 365–381.

[134] M. Roemer, "Religion and Psychological Distress in Japan," *Social Forces* 89, no. 2 (2010): 559–583.

[135] V. Frankl, *Man's Search for Meaning* (Boston, MA: Beacon Press, 2006).

[136] J. Marston, "Meaning in Life: A Spiritual Matter—Projected Changes Post-retirement for Baby Boomers," *Journal of Religion, Spirituality & Aging* 22, no. 4 (2010): 329–342.

[137] E. Yoon et al., "Social Connectedness, Discrimination, and Social Status as Mediators of Acculturation/Enculturation and Well-being," *Journal of Counseling Psychology* (forthcoming), advance online publication, 05 September 2011.

[138] I. Mauss et al., "Don't Hide Your Happiness! Positive Emotion Dissociation, Social Connectedness, and Psychological Functioning," *Journal of Personality and Social Psychology* 31, January 2011, 1–11.

[139] H. Gray, K. Ishii, and N. Ambady, "Misery Loves Company: When Sadness Increases the Desire for Social Connectedness," *Personality and Social Psychology Bulletin,* 37, no. 11 (2011): 1438–1448.

[140] N. Mohatt et al., "Assessment of Awareness of Connectedness as a Culturally-based Protective Factor for Alaska Native Youth," *Cultural Diversity and Ethnic Minority Psychology* 17, no. 4 (2011): 444–455.

[141] J. DeKlerk, A. Boshoff, and R. Van Wyk, "Spirituality in Practice: Relationships Between Meaning in Life, Commitment, and Motivation," *Journal of Management, Spirituality & Religion* 3, no.4 (2006): 319–347.

[142] De Klerk, Boshoff, and Van Wyk, "Spirituality in Practice," 320.

[143] V. Frankl, *Man's Search for Meaning.*

Notes: Chapter Seven

[144] Explained by M. Martin, "Paradoxes of Happiness," *Journal of Happiness Studies* 9 (2008): 171–184.

[145] As suggested by K. Leyden, A. Goldberg, and P. Michelbach, "Understanding the Pursuit of Happiness in Ten Major Cities," *Urban Affairs Review* 47 (2011): 861–888.

[146] Leyden, Goldberg, and Michelbach, "Understanding the Pursuit of Happiness."

[147] D. Tovar-Murray, "The Multiple Determinants of Religious Behaviors and Spiritual Beliefs on Well-being," *Journal of Spirituality in Mental Health* 13, no. 3 (2011): 182–192.

[148] R. Walsh, "Lifestyle and Mental Health," *American Psychologist* 66, no. 7 (2011): 579–592.

Printed in the United States
By Bookmasters